HOW TO DRAW SUPERHEROES and SUPERVILLAINS

Illustrated by Jael

Copyright © 1994 Kidsbooks Inc.
3535 West Peterson Avenue
Chicago, IL 60659

Manufactured in the United States of America

INTRODUCTION

This book will show you how to draw lots of different superheroes and supervillains. Some are more difficult than others, but if you follow along, step-by-step, you'll soon be able to draw any hero or villain you wish.

Each figure in this book begins with a **line or stick figure**. This establishes the direction or movement of the character to be drawn. Then, different kinds of **oval** shapes are added over the line figure to round out the basic sections of the body. Variations of ovals and other basic shapes will also be used.

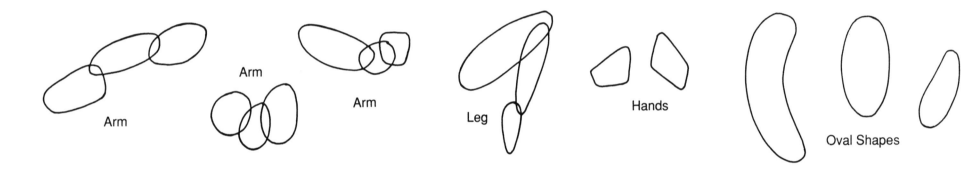

Arm

Arm

Arm

Leg

Hands

Oval Shapes

Note: The basic shapes usually overlap when forming the arms and legs.

The first two steps of each drawing look easy, but they are the most important. It's here that you create a **solid foundation** of the figure — much like a builder who must first construct a foundation before building the rest of the house. If the foundation of your drawing is solid, you'll quickly get to the fun part — creating the muscles, face, clothing, and weapons, and adding all the details and finishing touches.

SUPPLIES

NUMBER 2 PENCILS
SOFT ERASER
DRAWING PAD
FELT-TIP PEN
COLORED PENCILS, MARKERS,
OR CRAYONS

HELPFUL HINTS

1. Following the **first two steps** carefully will make the final steps easier.
2. **Always keep your pencil lines light and soft**. These "guide-lines" will be easier to erase when you no longer need them.
3. **Don't be afraid to erase.** It usually takes lots of drawing and erasing before you will be satisfied with the way your superhero or supervillain looks.

4. Add details and all the finishing touches **after** you have blended and refined all the shapes and your figure is complete.
5. You can check a pose by using yourself as a model. Just stand in front of a full-length mirror.
6. Remember: **Practice Makes Perfect.** Don't be discouraged if you can't get the "hang of it" right away. Just keep drawing and erasing until you do.

Foreshortening

Superheroes and supervillains are shown in dramatic poses that use **foreshortening**. To understand this better, stand in front of a mirror and point to yourself with one arm. See how short your arm appears? Then hold your other arm straight out to your side. Now you can see your arm's normal length. An artist learns to draw things as the eye sees them, not as they really are. This gives the figure a realistic, 3-dimensional appearance.

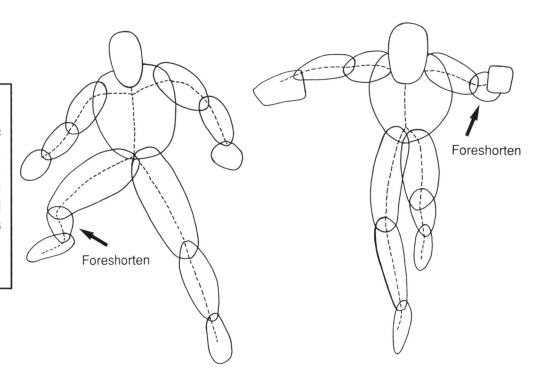

Foreshorten

Foreshorten

HOW TO START

Before starting your first drawing, you may want to practice tracing the different steps.

1. Begin by drawing a stick figure like the one on this page. This will help you make the figure move in the right direction. The action and movement of a figure is called **gesture.**

2. Carefully add the oval shapes to the stick figure. Note that many of these ovals are not "perfect" and that they overlap. These are the basic guidelines that form the body and create the foundation.

REMEMBER TO KEEP YOUR GUIDELINES LIGHTLY DRAWN

3. Carefully draw the body muscles **within** the oval guidelines. The dotted lines show what can be erased. As you begin to connect and blend the shapes together, start erasing the stick figure and any other guidelines that you no longer need. Keep drawing and erasing until you're satisfied with the way your drawing looks **before** adding the final touches.

4. Add facial features, hair, clothing, and all the other details and finishing touches to complete your drawing. Color your finished superhero or supervillain with your favorite colors or, for a more dramatic effect, outline them with a thick, black marker.

Elsewhere in this book you will find illustrations of weapons, futuristic cities, and additional characters. These are just **examples** of things you can add to a finished picture. Once you've mastered the basic drawing technique, use your **imagination** and create different objects and backgrounds to enhance your drawings.

When you have drawn some or all of the characters in this book, and are comfortable with the drawing technique, start creating **your own** superheroes and supervillains.

Most of all, **HAVE FUN!**

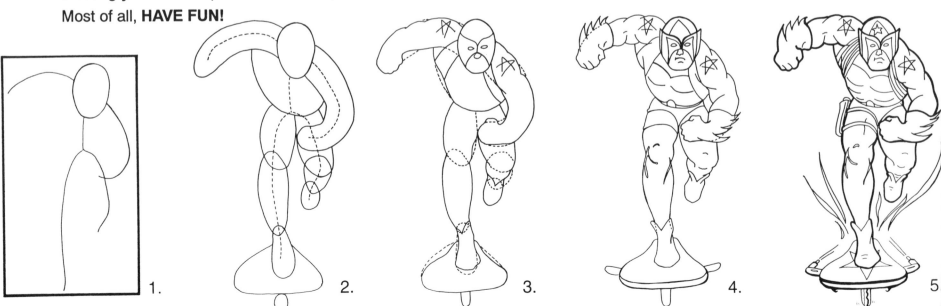

1.   2.   3.   4.   5

HOW TO DRAW SUPERHEROES

Illustrated by Jael

BLADE RIDER

3. Start defining and shaping the muscles within the oval guidelines, erasing your gesture lines as you go along. Then, begin outlining this superhero's hair, hands, and face.

1.

2.

1.& 2. Starting with the head, draw the simple stick figure (gesture lines). Then add the various ovals and other guideline shapes.

Use foreshortening when any part of the body points away from or toward, you, the viewer. This gives your figure a dramatic, 3-dimensional look.

Note: Keep all your guidelines lightly drawn. They will be easier to erase later on.

Before going to the next step, make sure that you are satisfied with the way your drawing looks.

5. Now add all the final details and finishing touches, and Blade Rider is ready for action!

4. Complete the facial features and sharply define Blade Rider's arms, legs, and chest muscles. Then, begin adding clothes and details.

BOLT-MAN

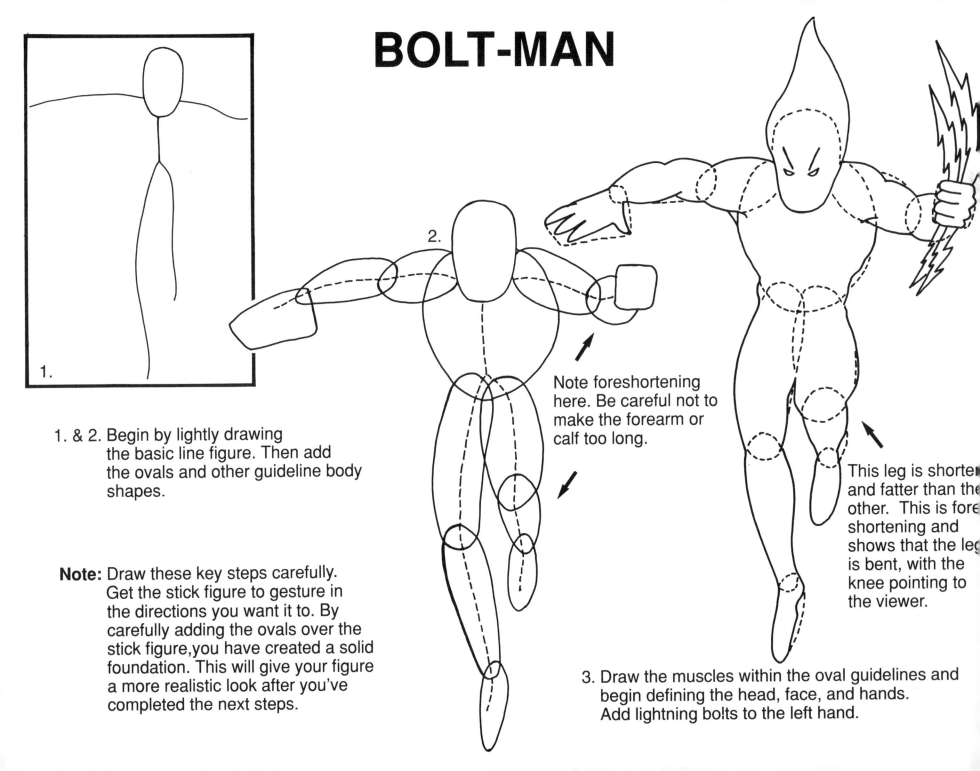

1.

2.

Note foreshortening here. Be careful not to make the forearm or calf too long.

1. & 2. Begin by lightly drawing the basic line figure. Then add the ovals and other guideline body shapes.

Note: Draw these key steps carefully. Get the stick figure to gesture in the directions you want it to. By carefully adding the ovals over the stick figure, you have created a solid foundation. This will give your figure a more realistic look after you've completed the next steps.

This leg is shorter and fatter than the other. This is foreshortening and shows that the leg is bent, with the knee pointing to the viewer.

3. Draw the muscles within the oval guidelines and begin defining the head, face, and hands. Add lightning bolts to the left hand.

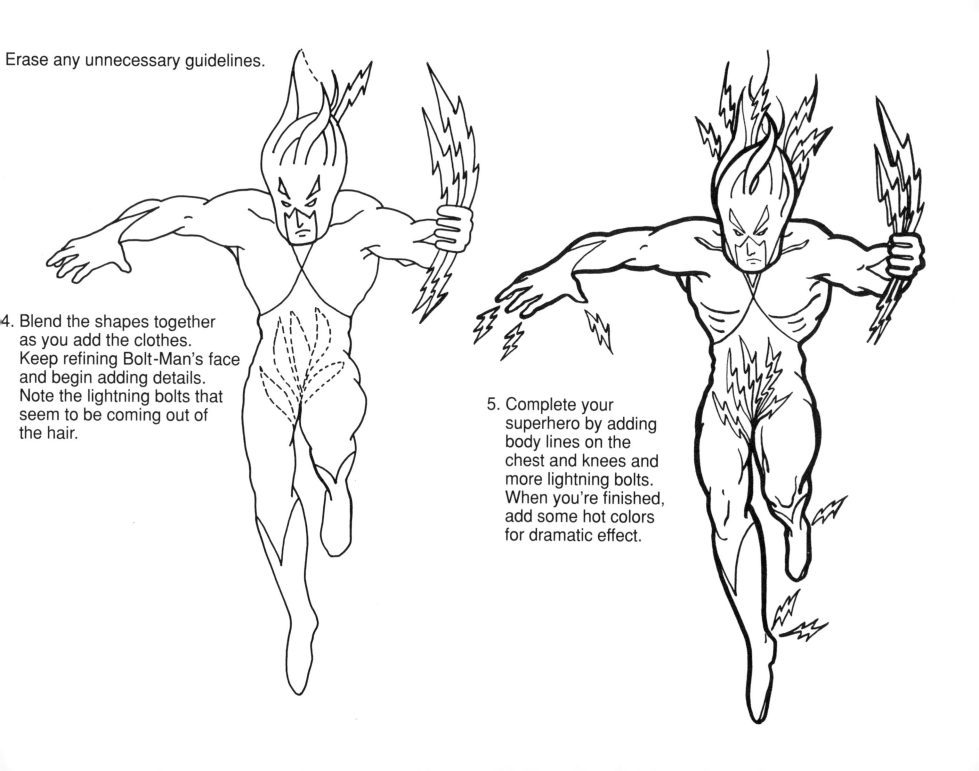

Erase any unnecessary guidelines.

4. Blend the shapes together
as you add the clothes.
Keep refining Bolt-Man's face
and begin adding details.
Note the lightning bolts that
seem to be coming out of
the hair.

5. Complete your
superhero by adding
body lines on the
chest and knees and
more lightning bolts.
When you're finished,
add some hot colors
for dramatic effect.

LEKTRA

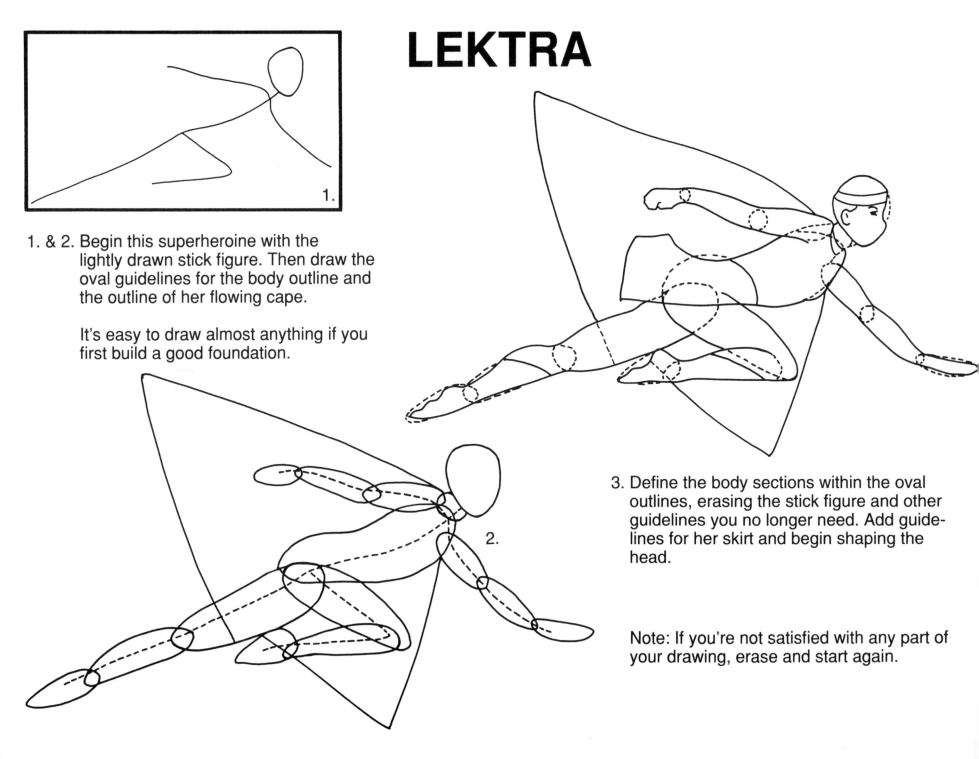

1. & 2. Begin this superheroine with the lightly drawn stick figure. Then draw the oval guidelines for the body outline and the outline of her flowing cape.

It's easy to draw almost anything if you first build a good foundation.

3. Define the body sections within the oval outlines, erasing the stick figure and other guidelines you no longer need. Add guidelines for her skirt and begin shaping the head.

Note: If you're not satisfied with any part of your drawing, erase and start again.

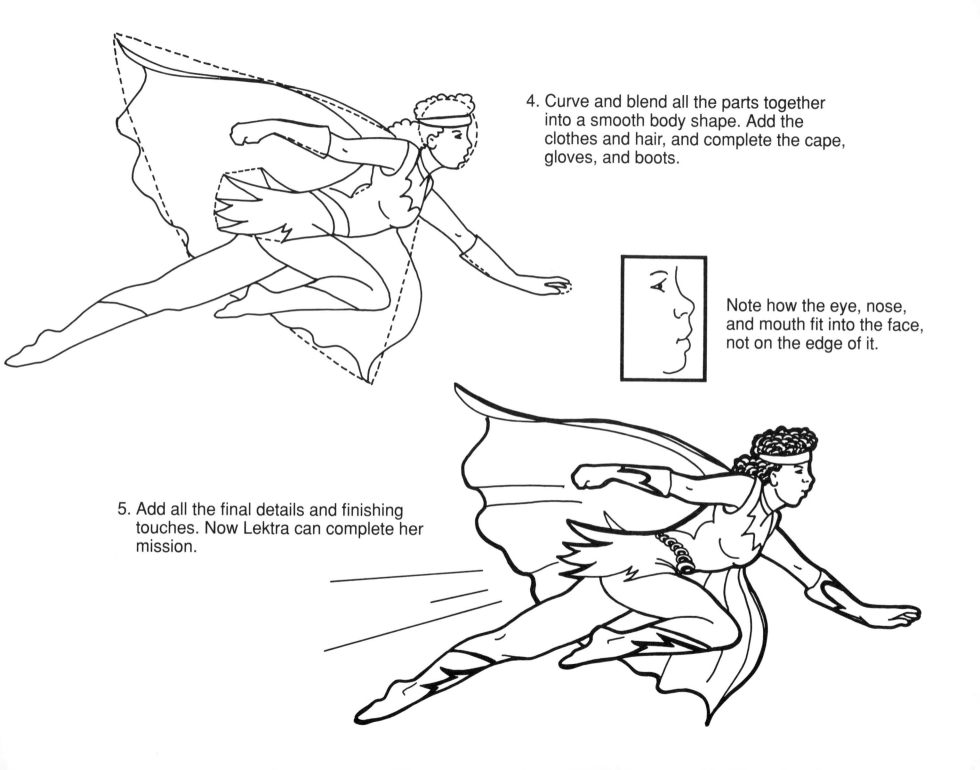

4. Curve and blend all the parts together into a smooth body shape. Add the clothes and hair, and complete the cape, gloves, and boots.

Note how the eye, nose, and mouth fit into the face, not on the edge of it.

5. Add all the final details and finishing touches. Now Lektra can complete her mission.

ROBO-MAN

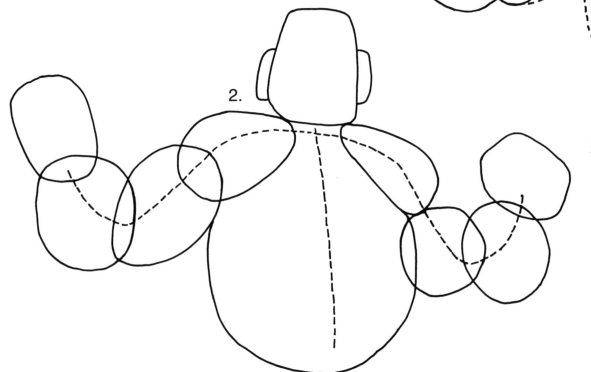

1.

1. & 2. Draw the gesture lines. Then add the guideline shapes for the head, arms, and torso.

2.

3. Draw the simple shapes on Robo-Man's face and carefully add the fingers. Define the torso and arm sections, erasing any unnecessary guidelines as you go along.

Remember to keep all your guidelines lightly drawn, so that they may be easily erased.

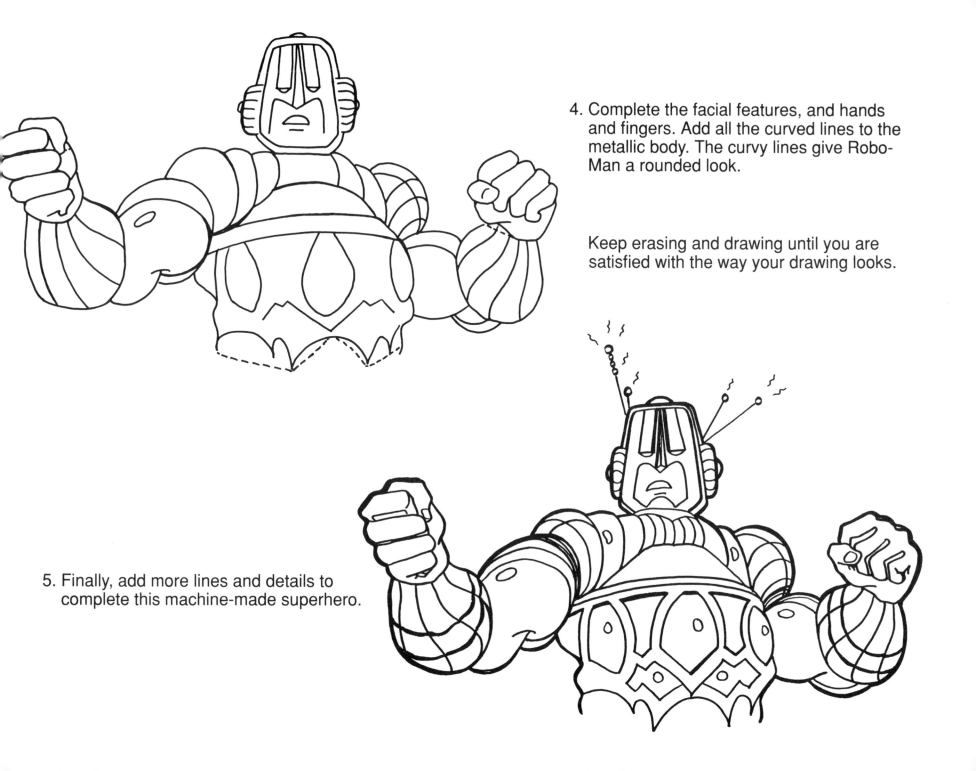

4. Complete the facial features, and hands and fingers. Add all the curved lines to the metallic body. The curvy lines give Robo-Man a rounded look.

Keep erasing and drawing until you are satisfied with the way your drawing looks.

5. Finally, add more lines and details to complete this machine-made superhero.

ZANTRON

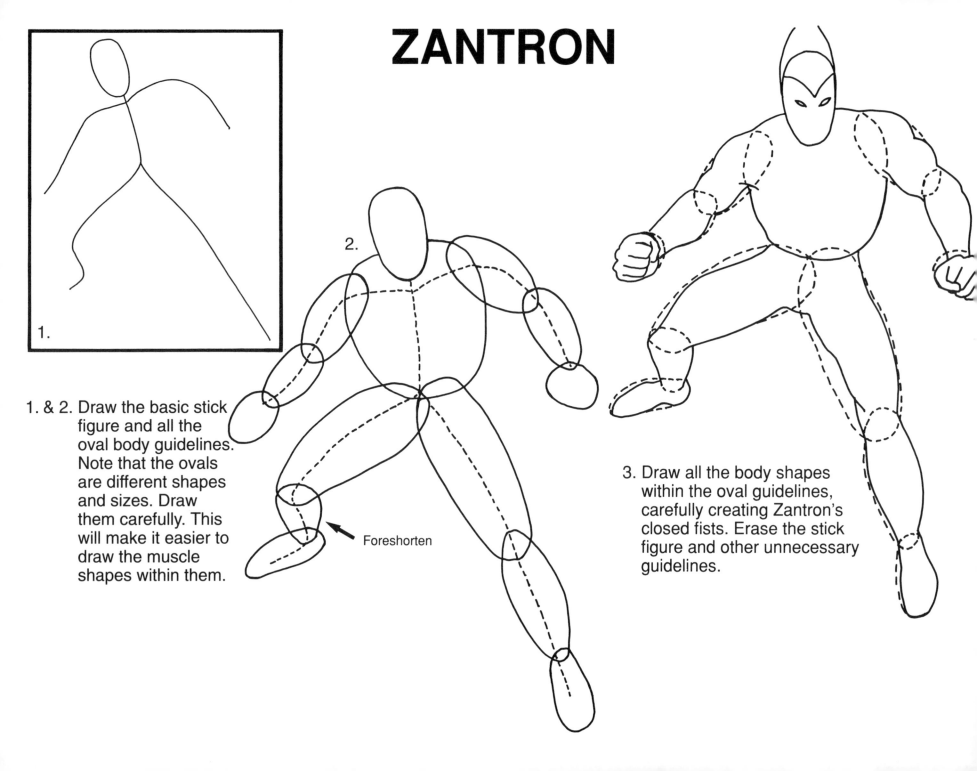

1.

2.

Foreshorten

1. & 2. Draw the basic stick figure and all the oval body guidelines. Note that the ovals are different shapes and sizes. Draw them carefully. This will make it easier to draw the muscle shapes within them.

3. Draw all the body shapes within the oval guidelines, carefully creating Zantron's closed fists. Erase the stick figure and other unnecessary guidelines.

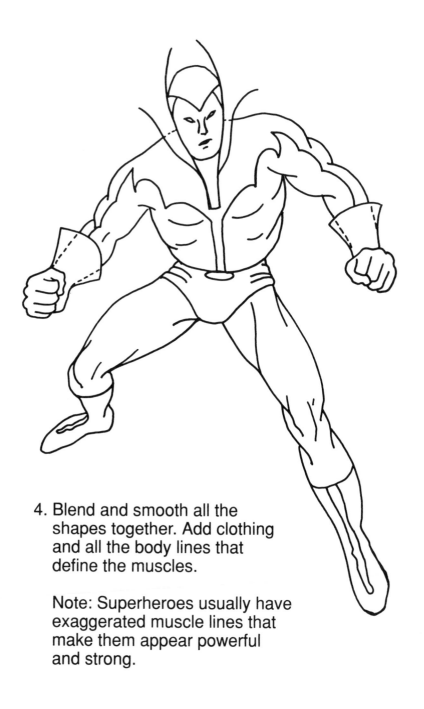

4. Blend and smooth all the shapes together. Add clothing and all the body lines that define the muscles.

Note: Superheroes usually have exaggerated muscle lines that make them appear powerful and strong.

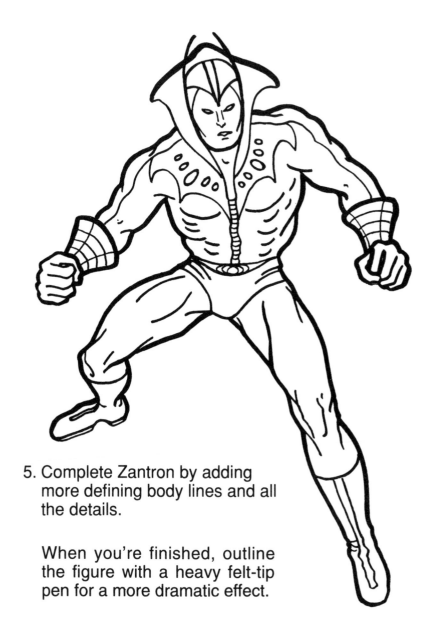

5. Complete Zantron by adding more defining body lines and all the details.

When you're finished, outline the figure with a heavy felt-tip pen for a more dramatic effect.

ZEPHRA

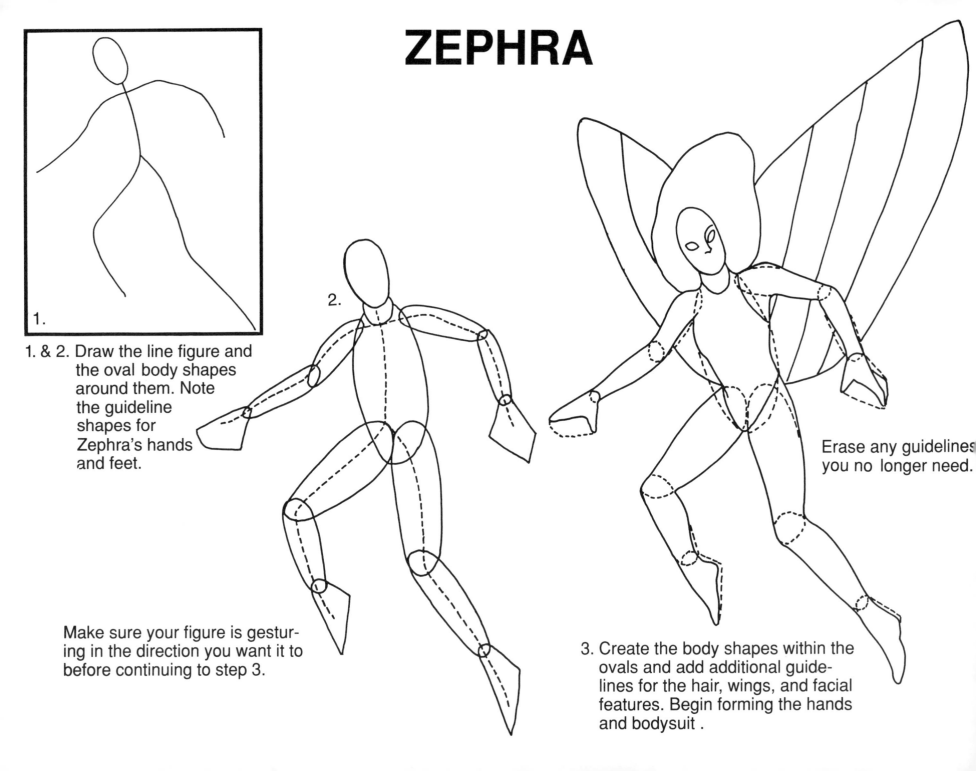

1.

1. & 2. Draw the line figure and the oval body shapes around them. Note the guideline shapes for Zephra's hands and feet.

Make sure your figure is gesturing in the direction you want it to before continuing to step 3.

2.

Erase any guidelines you no longer need.

3. Create the body shapes within the ovals and add additional guidelines for the hair, wings, and facial features. Begin forming the hands and bodysuit .

4. Blend the body parts together; complete the facial features; and finish drawing the hands. Zephra has beautiful, feathered wings. Starting close to her body — from the inside out — draw the feathers. Lastly, draw her flowing, wavy hair and begin adding details to her outfit.

Draw rows of overlapping semi-oval shapes for the feathers.

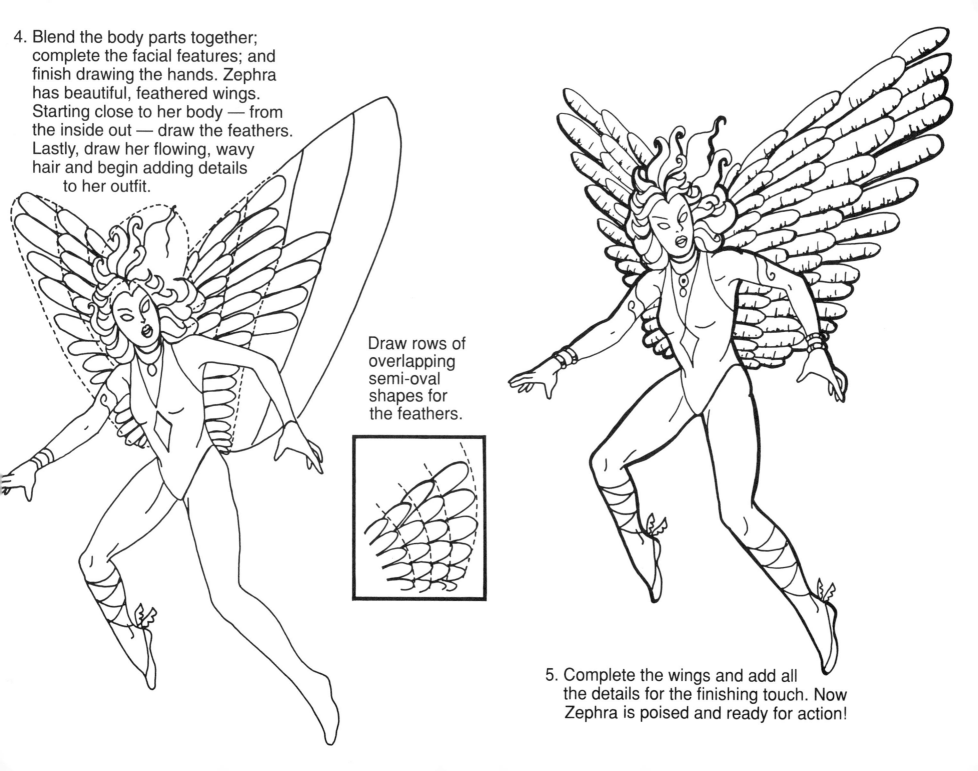

5. Complete the wings and add all the details for the finishing touch. Now Zephra is poised and ready for action!

KARZAN AND ZAP

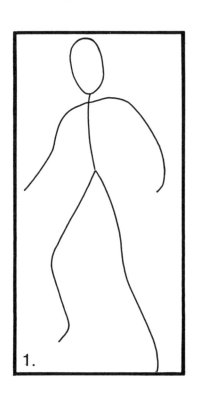

1. & 2. Lightly draw the stick figure and all the oval guideline shapes around it. This superhero has a friendly reptile, named Zap, for a sidekick. Add the two overlapping guideline shapes for the reptile.

3. First, lightly sketch Karzan's muscular body parts within the oval shapes, paying careful attention to the hands. Add the knife, eyes and nose, loincloth, and guides for the hairline. Next, add the guideline shapes on the superhero's sidekick, as shown. Erase any lines you no longer need.

4. Blend the shapes into a smooth, muscular body. Add the boots, bow, arrow holder, facial features, and hair. Now start working on the smiling reptile. Create the wavy plate on Zap's back and the curved teeth and claws.

5. Add the remaining details, and Karzan and Zap are ready to face the unknown.

To draw scales:
Following the natural curves of the body, lightly draw the guideline rows, as shown. Then fill in each row with overlapping scales.

QUASAR-MAN

1.

1. & 2. Starting with the oval-shaped head, draw the stick figure. Add the broad body shapes for the super muscles, and the board beneath the right foot.

Remember to keep these guidelines lightly drawn.

2.

3. Create all the parts of Quasar-man's body within the guideline shapes. Add guidelines for his facial features and mask, erasing any lines you no longer need as you go along. As this super-hero lunges forward, note how his chest and uplifted left leg are foreshortened.

Note: Step 3 is a very important step. It establishes the basic overall structure and look of your drawing. In steps 4 and 5, you are simply refining and adding details to the figure you have created.

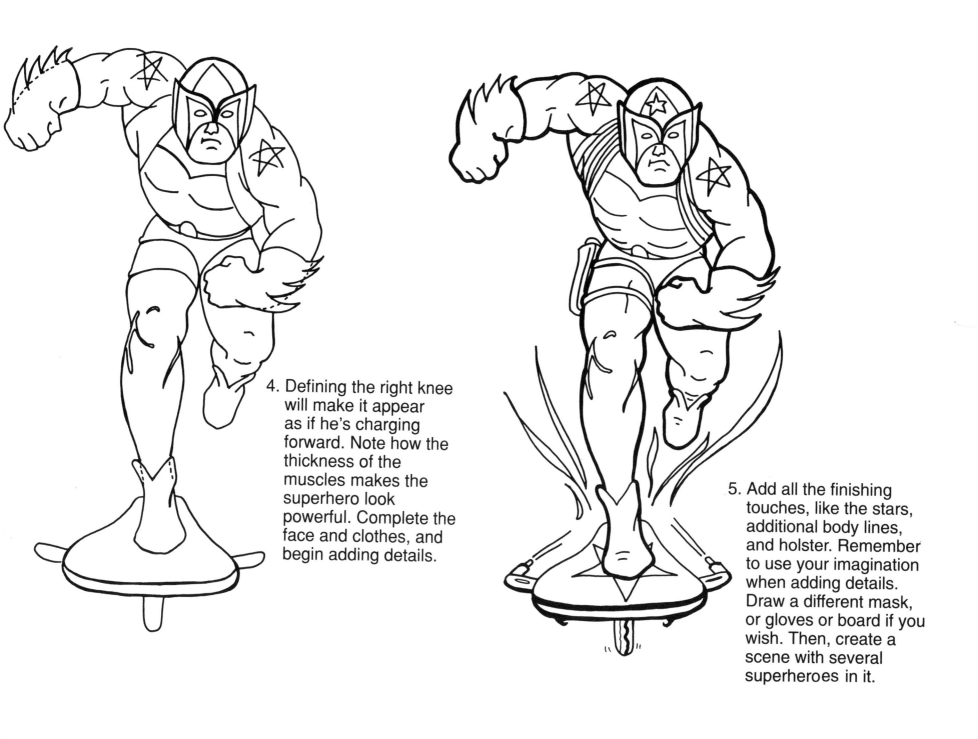

4. Defining the right knee will make it appear as if he's charging forward. Note how the thickness of the muscles makes the superhero look powerful. Complete the face and clothes, and begin adding details.

5. Add all the finishing touches, like the stars, additional body lines, and holster. Remember to use your imagination when adding details. Draw a different mask, or gloves or board if you wish. Then, create a scene with several superheroes in it.

GIGANTO

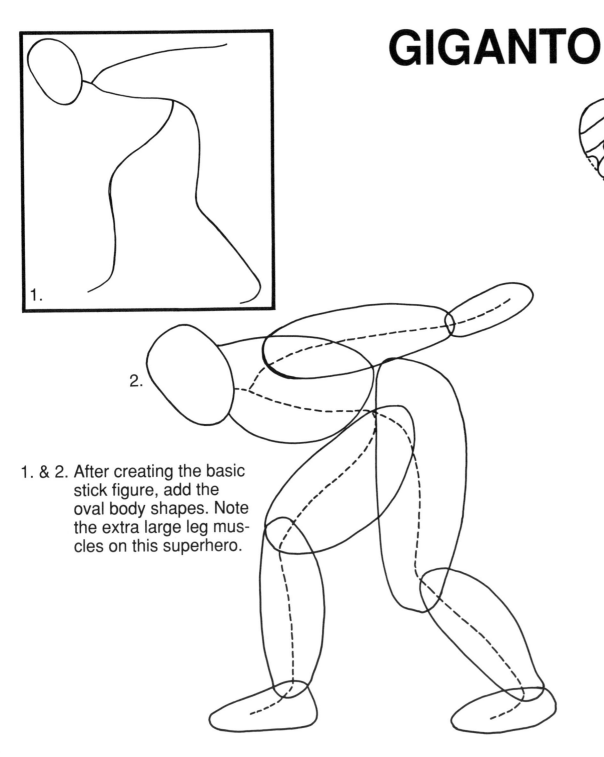

1.

2.

1. & 2. After creating the basic stick figure, add the oval body shapes. Note the extra large leg muscles on this superhero.

3. Draw the muscles within the oval shapes. Add guidelines for the facial features and begin defining the feet.

Erase the stick figure and the other guidelines that are no longer needed.

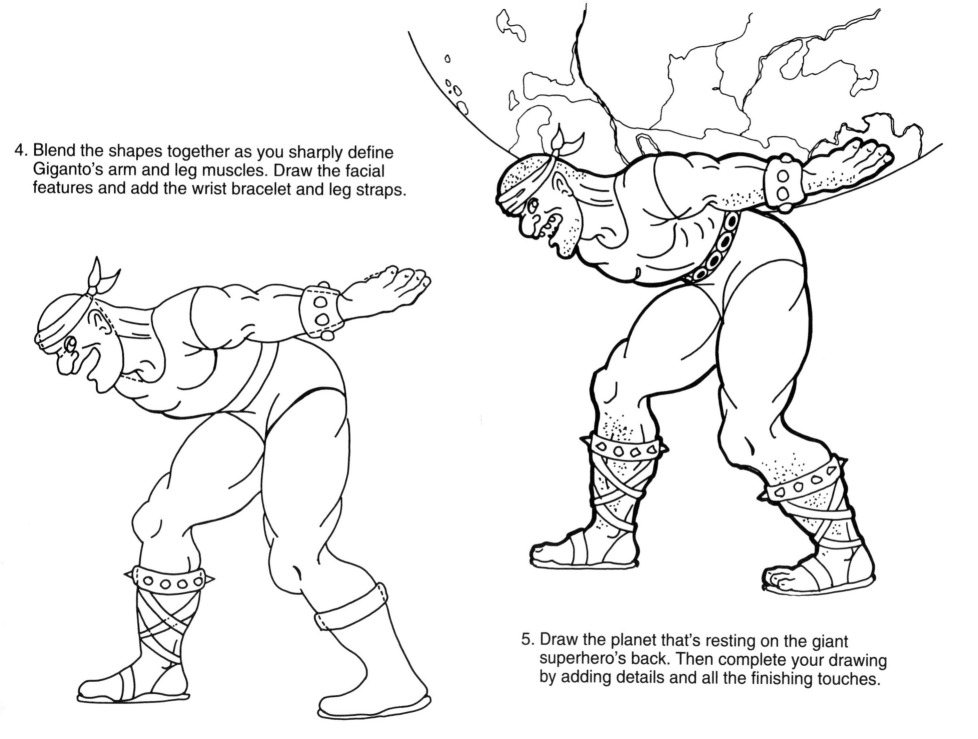

4. Blend the shapes together as you sharply define Giganto's arm and leg muscles. Draw the facial features and add the wrist bracelet and leg straps.

5. Draw the planet that's resting on the giant superhero's back. Then complete your drawing by adding details and all the finishing touches.

TRANSFLIER

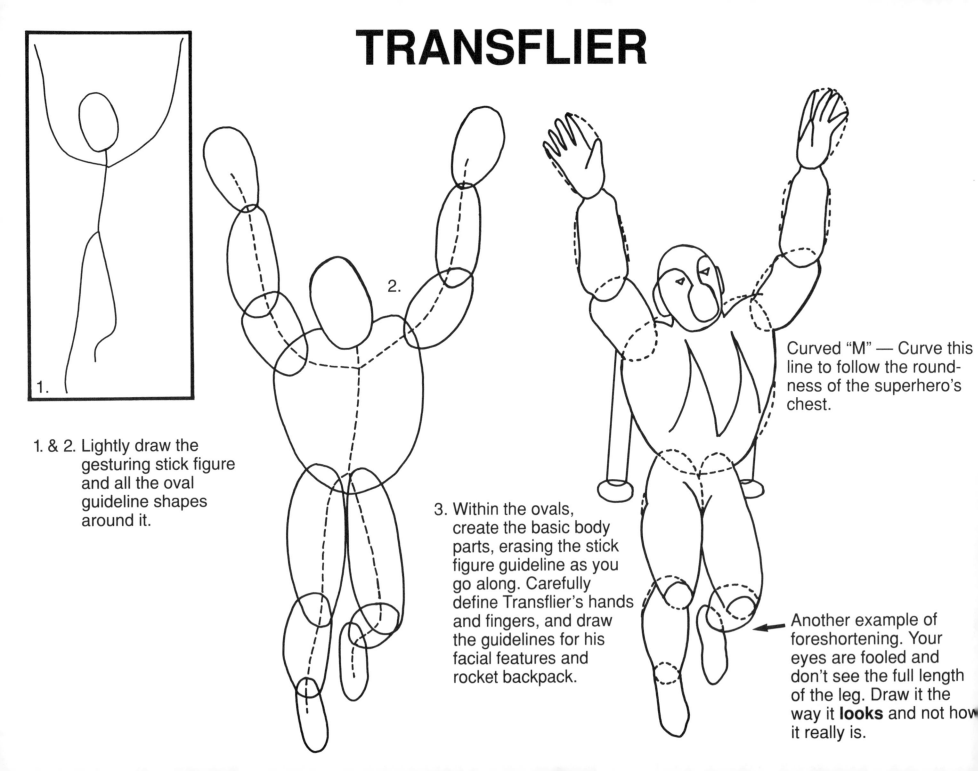

1.

2.

1. & 2. Lightly draw the gesturing stick figure and all the oval guideline shapes around it.

3. Within the ovals, create the basic body parts, erasing the stick figure guideline as you go along. Carefully define Transflier's hands and fingers, and draw the guidelines for his facial features and rocket backpack.

Curved "M" — Curve this line to follow the roundness of the superhero's chest.

Another example of foreshortening. Your eyes are fooled and don't see the full length of the leg. Draw it the way it **looks** and not how it really is.

4. Blend and shape all the forms together, paying close attention to the curved lines on the arms and legs. Continue working on the face and fingers, and begin adding details.

5. Add lots more details to complete Transflier. When you're finished, add exhaust lines to the rocket so that he can zoom away.

STEELO
THE ULTIMATE

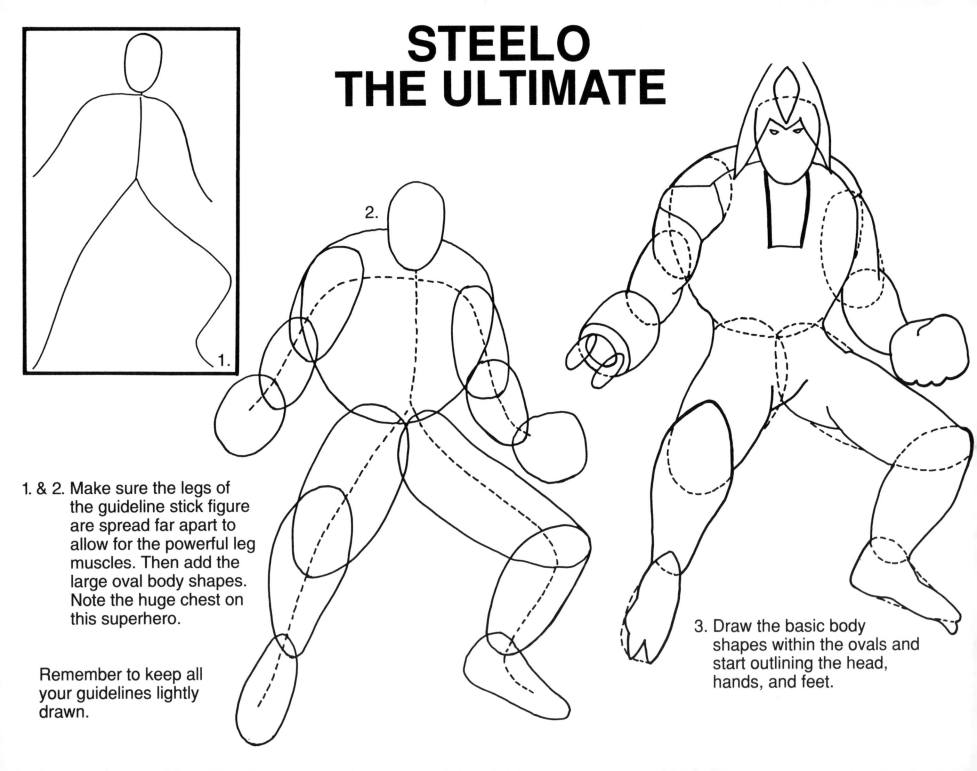

1. & 2. Make sure the legs of the guideline stick figure are spread far apart to allow for the powerful leg muscles. Then add the large oval body shapes. Note the huge chest on this superhero.

Remember to keep all your guidelines lightly drawn.

3. Draw the basic body shapes within the ovals and start outlining the head, hands, and feet.

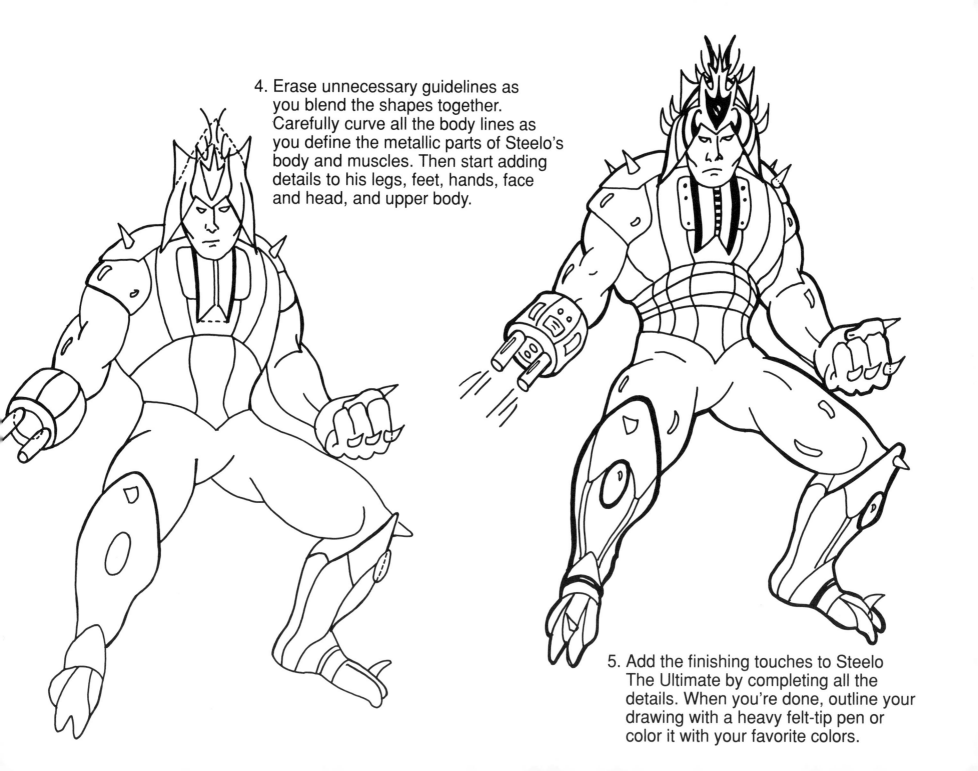

4. Erase unnecessary guidelines as you blend the shapes together. Carefully curve all the body lines as you define the metallic parts of Steelo's body and muscles. Then start adding details to his legs, feet, hands, face and head, and upper body.

5. Add the finishing touches to Steelo The Ultimate by completing all the details. When you're done, outline your drawing with a heavy felt-tip pen or color it with your favorite colors.

THORA

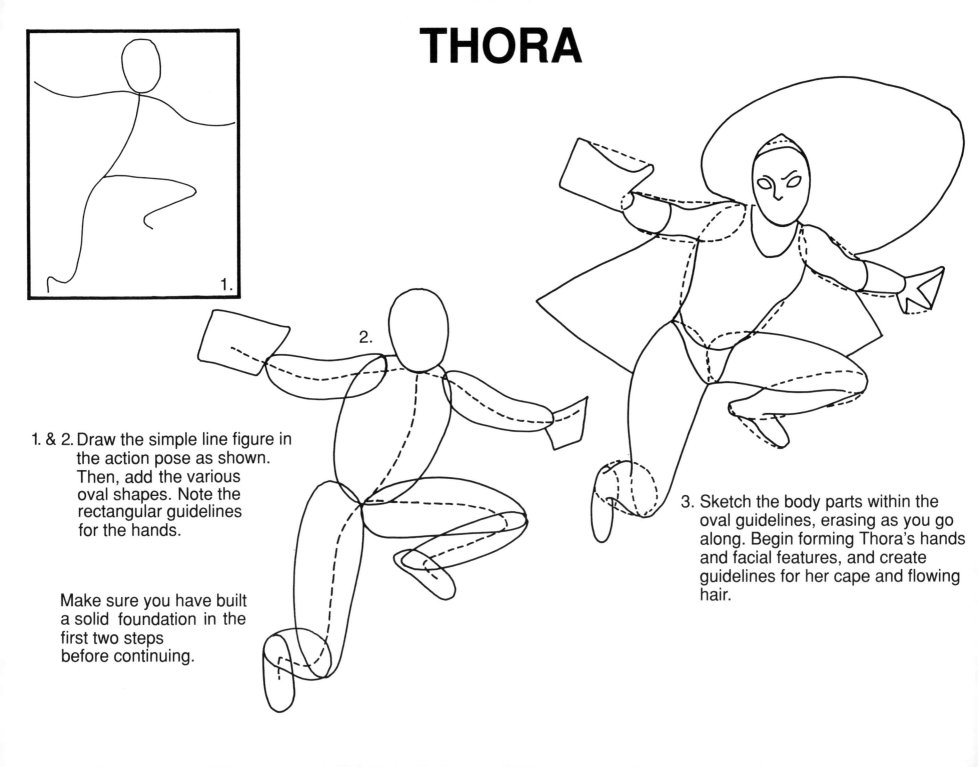

1. & 2. Draw the simple line figure in the action pose as shown. Then, add the various oval shapes. Note the rectangular guidelines for the hands.

Make sure you have built a solid foundation in the first two steps before continuing.

3. Sketch the body parts within the oval guidelines, erasing as you go along. Begin forming Thora's hands and facial features, and create guidelines for her cape and flowing hair.

5. Finish Thora's hair and cape, and add all the final details that will make this superheroine ready to spring into action.

4. Blend the body shapes together and complete the hands and face. Then, start forming her cape and long, flowing hair.

If you're not satisfied with the way any part of your drawing looks, erase it and start again.

CAPTAIN CRIMSON

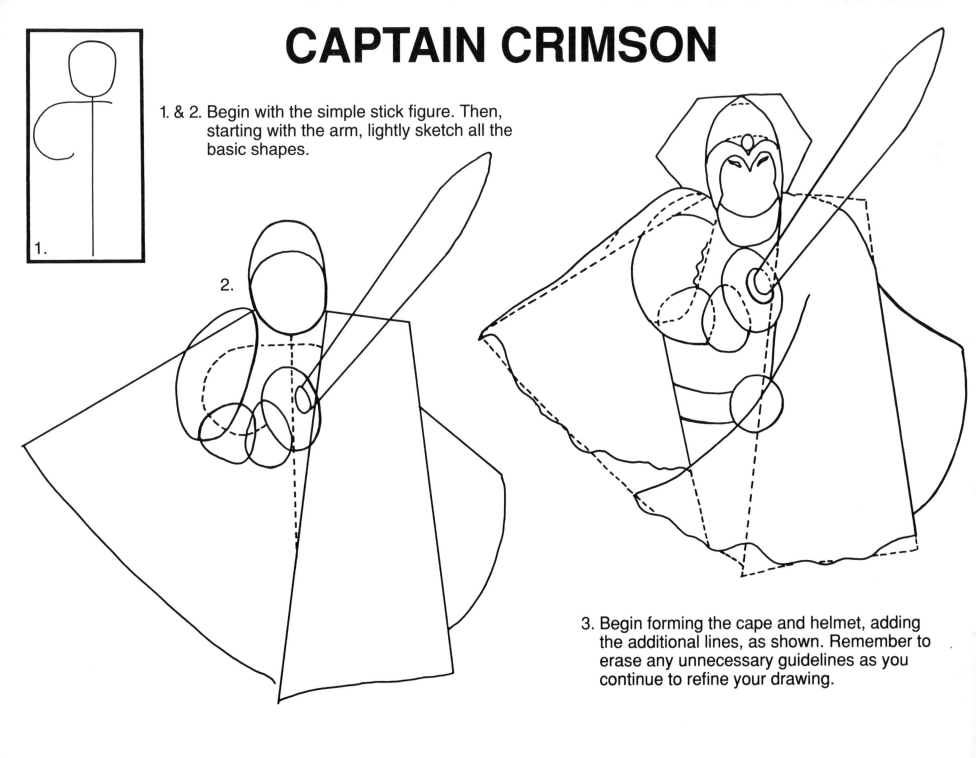

1. & 2. Begin with the simple stick figure. Then, starting with the arm, lightly sketch all the basic shapes.

3. Begin forming the cape and helmet, adding the additional lines, as shown. Remember to erase any unnecessary guidelines as you continue to refine your drawing.

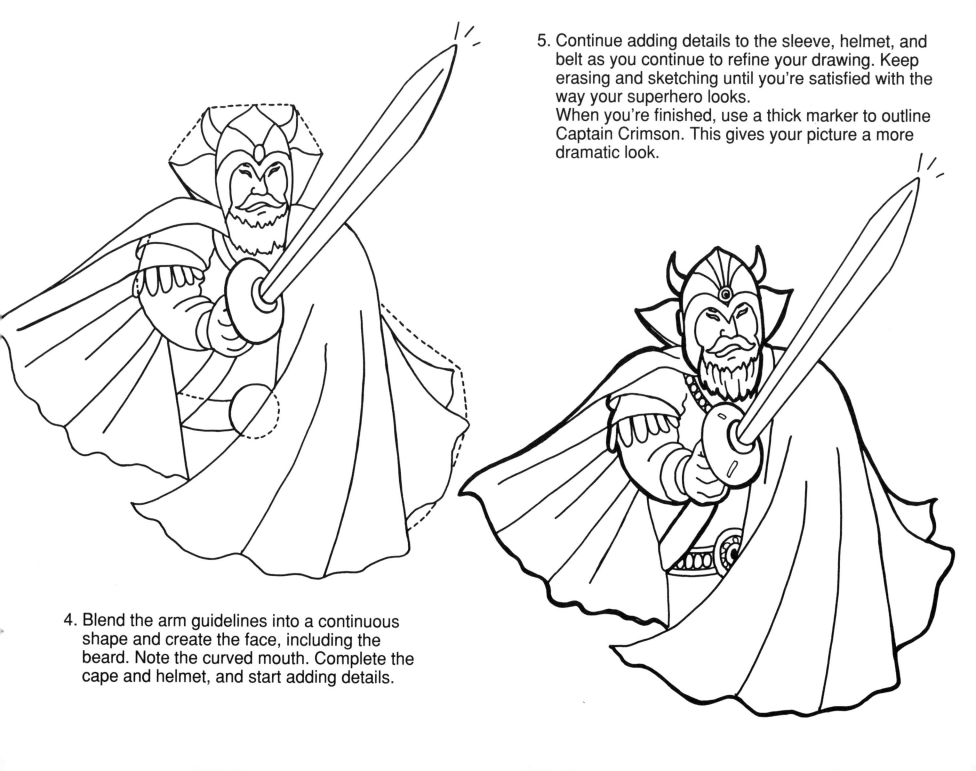

5. Continue adding details to the sleeve, helmet, and belt as you continue to refine your drawing. Keep erasing and sketching until you're satisfied with the way your superhero looks.

When you're finished, use a thick marker to outline Captain Crimson. This gives your picture a more dramatic look.

4. Blend the arm guidelines into a continuous shape and create the face, including the beard. Note the curved mouth. Complete the cape and helmet, and start adding details.

Here are a few examples of the kind of city a superhero might
come from. Try drawing these, then use your imagination to create others.
Backgrounds will give your drawing a "finished" look.

Another futuristic city on a distant planet.

These are just a few of the weapons, masks,
shields, etc., that you can add to any of your superhero drawings.
Use your imagination and create many more.

HOW TO DRAW SUPERVILLAINS

Illustrated by Jael

THAWRO, THE ICE BREAKER

3. Start defining and shaping the muscles within the oval guidelines, erasing your gesture lines as you go along. Then, begin outlining this supervillain's hands and facial features.

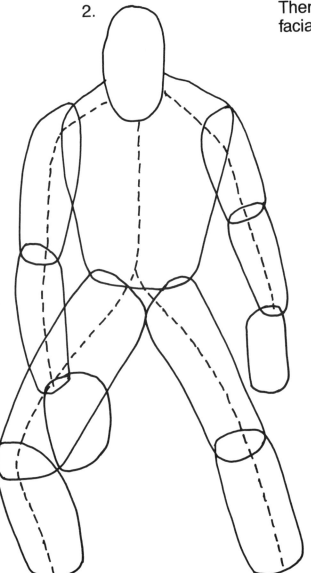

2.

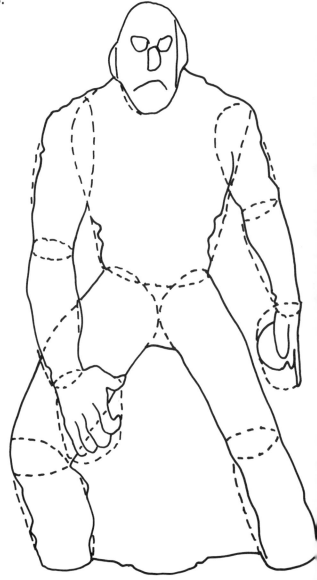

1. & 2. Starting with the head, draw the simple stick figure (gesture lines). Then add the various overlapping ovals and other guideline shapes.

Note: Keep all your guidelines lightly drawn. They will be easier to erase later on.

4. Erase any guidelines you no longer need and begin adding melting drops of water to Thawro.

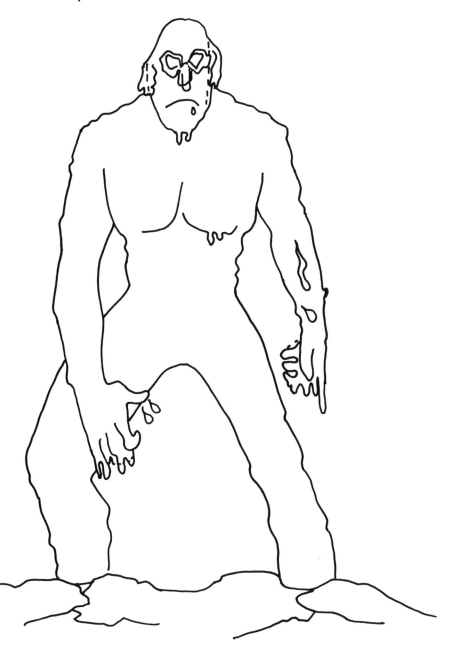

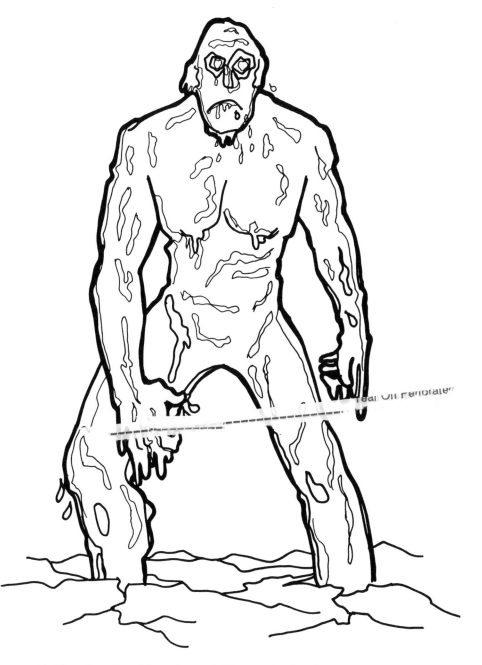

5. For the final touch, add lots of wiggly, squiggly, shapes all over the figure to make it look as if this transparent ice breaker is reflecting light.

FANG-FIEND

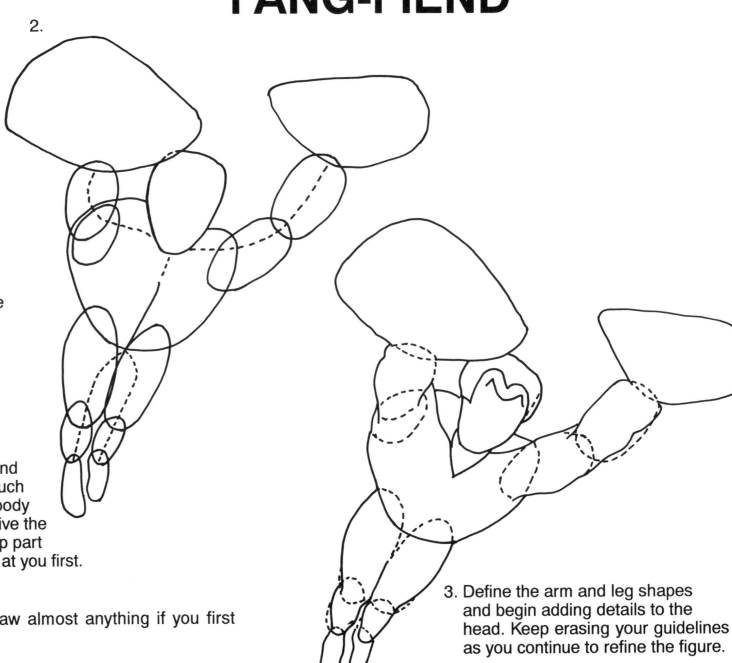

1.

2.

3.

1. & 2. Begin by lightly
   drawing the basic line
   figure. Then add the
   ovals for all the body
   parts.

Note: Fang-Fiend's hands and
upper body appear much
larger than his lower body
and feet. This helps give the
impression that the top part
of the body is coming at you first.

Remember: It's easy to draw almost anything if you first
build a good foundation.

3. Define the arm and leg shapes
   and begin adding details to the
   head. Keep erasing your guidelines
   as you continue to refine the figure.

5. Add the clothes and all the final details to his face. Then use a felt-tip pen to complete your drawing. A heavy outline always adds a dramatic effect to your drawing. And don't forget this supervillain's horns!

4. Draw the hands, fingers, and pointy nails and blend all the body shapes together. Add the rest of the facial features and begin adding details.

Before going to the next step, make sure that you are satisfied with the way your drawing looks so far.

SLUG-UGH!

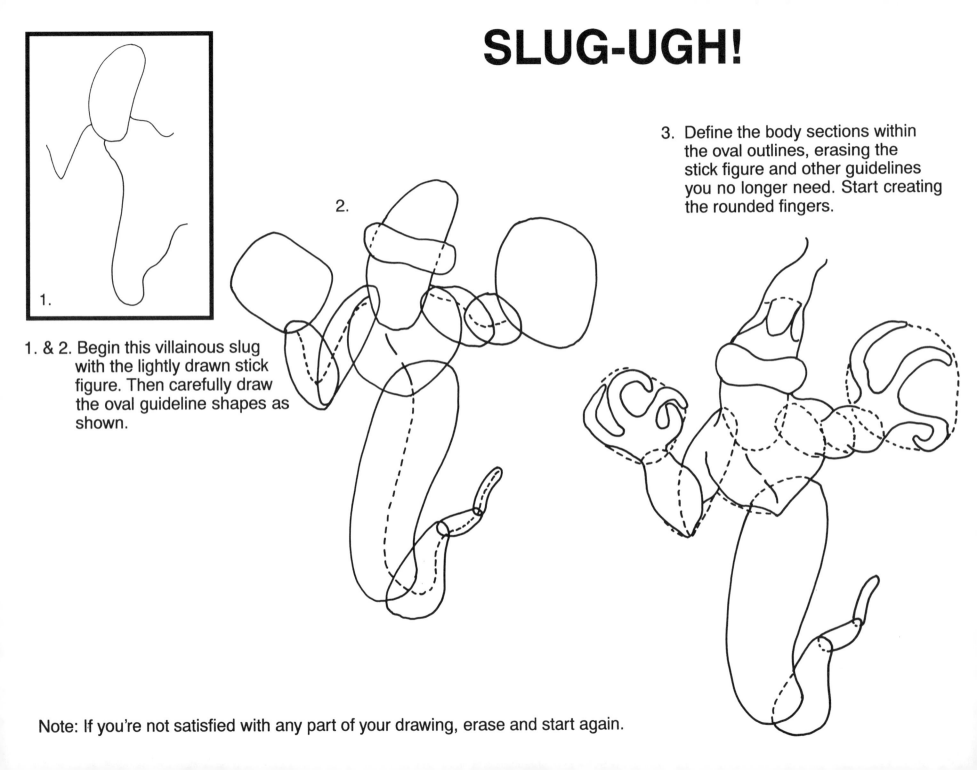

1.

1. & 2. Begin this villainous slug with the lightly drawn stick figure. Then carefully draw the oval guideline shapes as shown.

2.

3. Define the body sections within the oval outlines, erasing the stick figure and other guidelines you no longer need. Start creating the rounded fingers.

Note: If you're not satisfied with any part of your drawing, erase and start again.

5. Add the final details to the head and face and the other finishing touches. Now Slug-ugh! is ready to slither into mischief.

4. Curve and blend all the upper body shapes together and begin adding details to the face and head. For the lower body, start at the "waist" and draw a series of overlapping bands. Make each band smaller than the one before as you work your way down the tail.

CLUBERELLA

1. & 2. Draw the oval for the head and the gesture lines. Then add all the overlapping ovals for the arms, legs, and torso.

Note: Draw steps 1. and 2. carefully. Get the stick figure to gesture in the directions you want it to. By carefully adding the ovals over the stick figure, you have created a solid foundation and prepared your drawing for the final steps.

Remember to keep all your guidelines lightly drawn, so that they may be easily erased.

3. Add the club and start refining the body parts, erasing any unnecessary guidelines as you go along.

5. Finally, add all the finishing lines and details to complete this club-wielding supervillain.

4. Continue adding the various features, such as the hair, waist sash, face, hands, and clothing. Meanwhile, keep blending the parts together into a smooth body shape.

Keep erasing and drawing until you are satisfied with the way your drawing looks.

ISOR, THE CYBORG

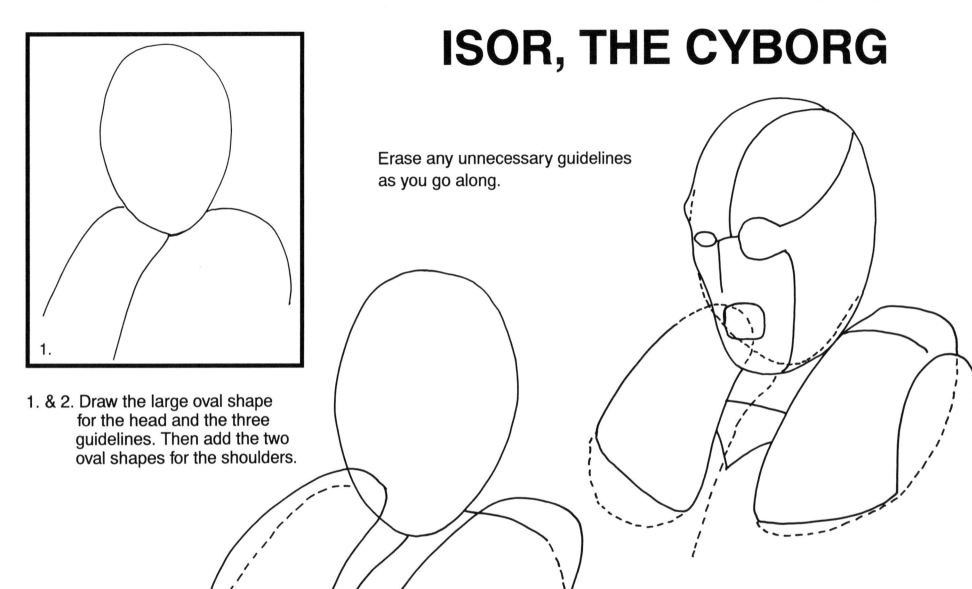

Erase any unnecessary guidelines as you go along.

1.

1. & 2. Draw the large oval shape for the head and the three guidelines. Then add the two oval shapes for the shoulders.

2.

3. Carefully add all the lines on the head as shown, and begin shaping the head and shoulders.

4. Blend and smooth all the shapes together. Add the beard and complete the facial features. Start adding headgear and other details.

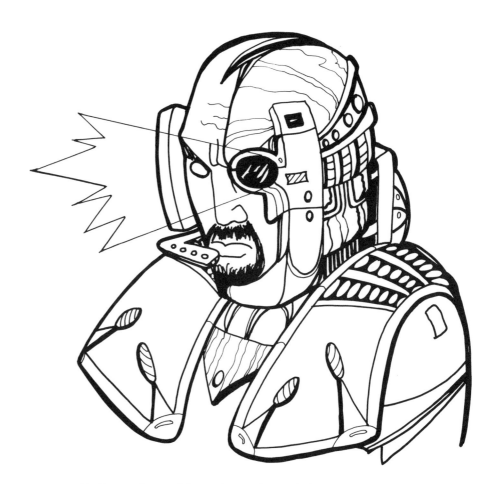

5. Complete this cyborg by adding lots of details to the head, headgear, and shoulder pads. Finally, draw the deadly x-ray shooting out from Isor's left eye.

ZAPATRON

Note: Supervillains have abnormally large muscle lines that make them appear powerful and dangerous.

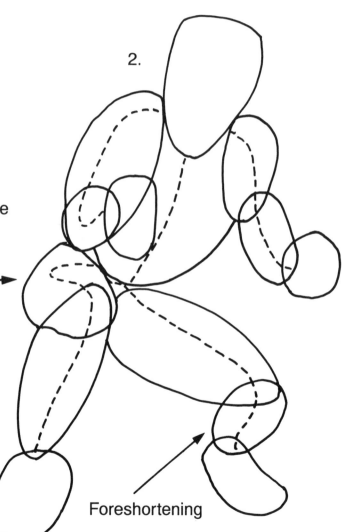

2.

1. & 2. Draw the standing line figure and the overlapping guideline body shapes.

Foreshortening →

Make sure your figure is gesturing in the direction you want it to before continuing to step 3.

Foreshortening

3. Create the body shapes within the ovals and add additional guidelines for the fingers, weapon, head, and facial features.

4. Blend Zapatron's body parts together and finish drawing his fingers and weapon. Begin adding details to the clothes and face.

Erase any guidelines you no longer need and when you're satisfied with the way your drawing looks, start adding the finishing touches.

5. Add all the final details to complete this supervillain. Use your imagination and add different bits and pieces to his clothing or to any other part of him.

Supervillains often have helpers, or sidekicks, in villainy to help them perform their mischievous deeds. Try to draw these few examples, adding them to your supervillain drawings. Then create your own characters.

Here are a few more "sidekicks" to add to your drawings.

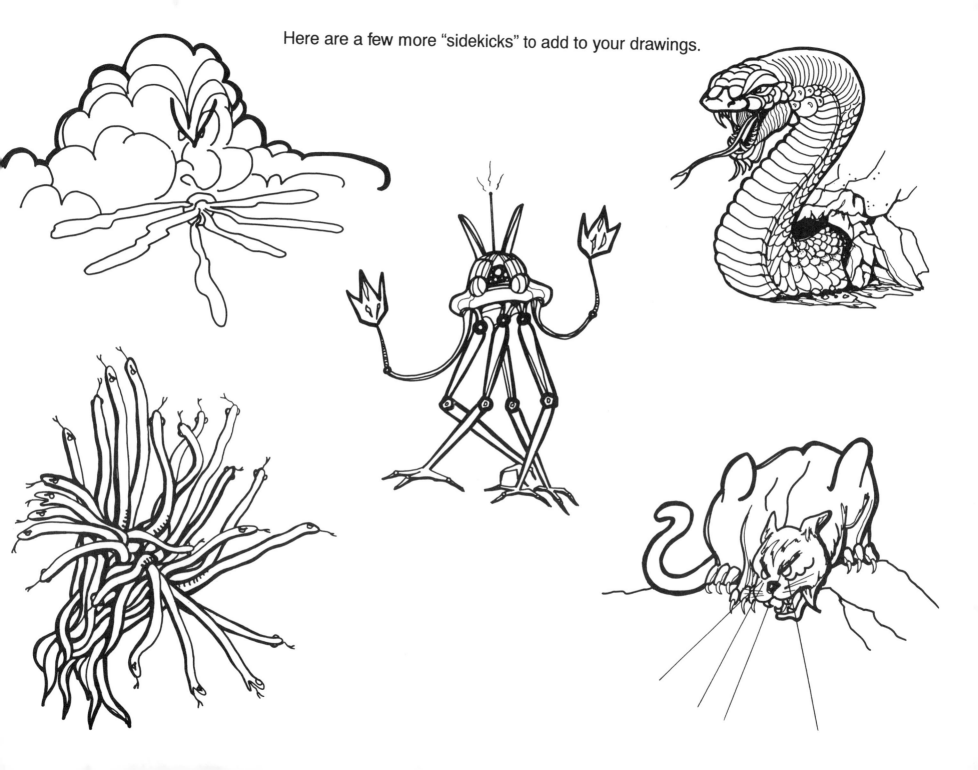

SCORCH THE TORCH

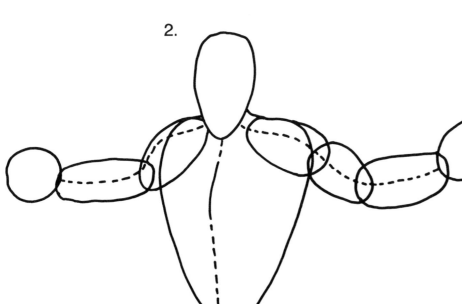

1. & 2. Draw the basic stick figure and all the overlapping ovals for the arms, hands, and torso.

Remember to keep these guidelines lightly drawn.

2.

3. Add additional guidelines as shown and begin shaping the arm sections and hands.

4. Finish the facial features, chest, arms, and hands. Begin adding flames to the face, head, and body. Blend all the shapes into a smooth outline, erasing any lines you no longer need as you go along.

5. Continue adding flames to this scorcher. Add lots of flames and make them shoot out as far as you like. Then create a scene with Scorch the Torch and several other supervillains in it.

THE ALIENATOR

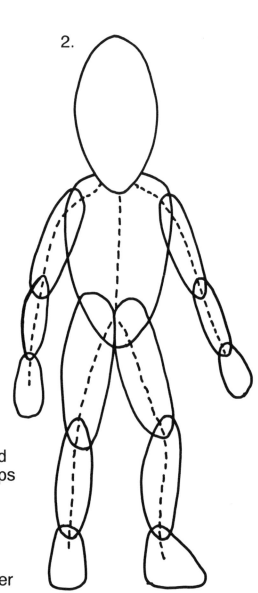

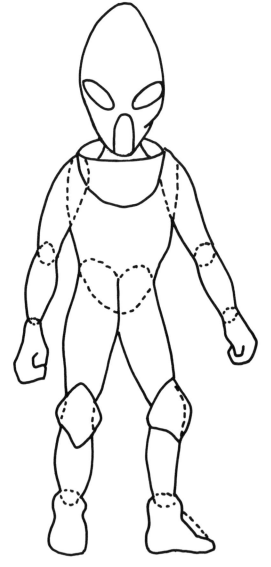

1. & 2. Starting with the oval-shaped head, draw the basic stick figure. Add the body ovals and shapes for the arms, legs, and torso.

Note: Make sure you have built a solid foundation with the first two steps before continuing.

Erase any guidelines that are no longer needed before going to the next step.

3. Erase the gesture lines and begin shaping and blending the ovals together. Add the boots, kneepads, facial guidelines, and collar. This little supervillain is beginning to take shape!

4. Add the long, pointy ears and finish the face. Complete the hands and start adding details to the clothes.

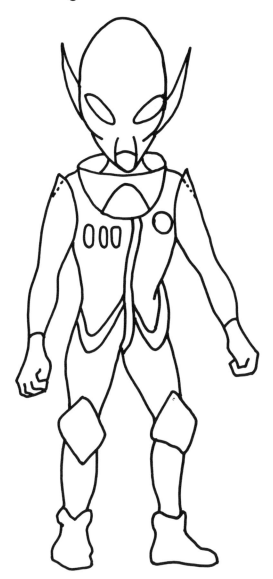

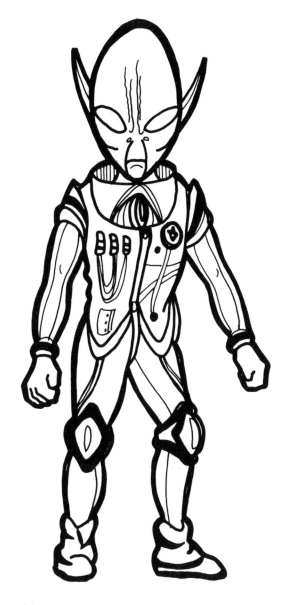

Remember: If you are not satisfied with the way any part of your drawing looks, erase it and start again.

5. Now complete your drawing by adding lots of details. For the finishing touches, add some of your favorite colors to your drawing. What color do you think the Alienator is?

DR. DESTRUCKTO

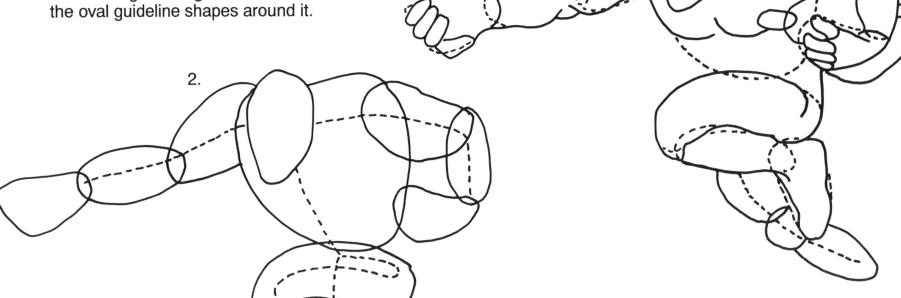

1. & 2. Lightly and carefully draw the "moving" stick figure and all the oval guideline shapes around it.

3. Within the ovals, create the basic body parts, erasing the stick figure as you go along. Carefully add the guideline shapes for his right leg. Start forming the fingers and facial features.

Note: This is a very important step. It establishes the basic overall structure and look of your drawing. In steps 4 and 5 you are simply refining and adding details to the figure you have created in step 3.

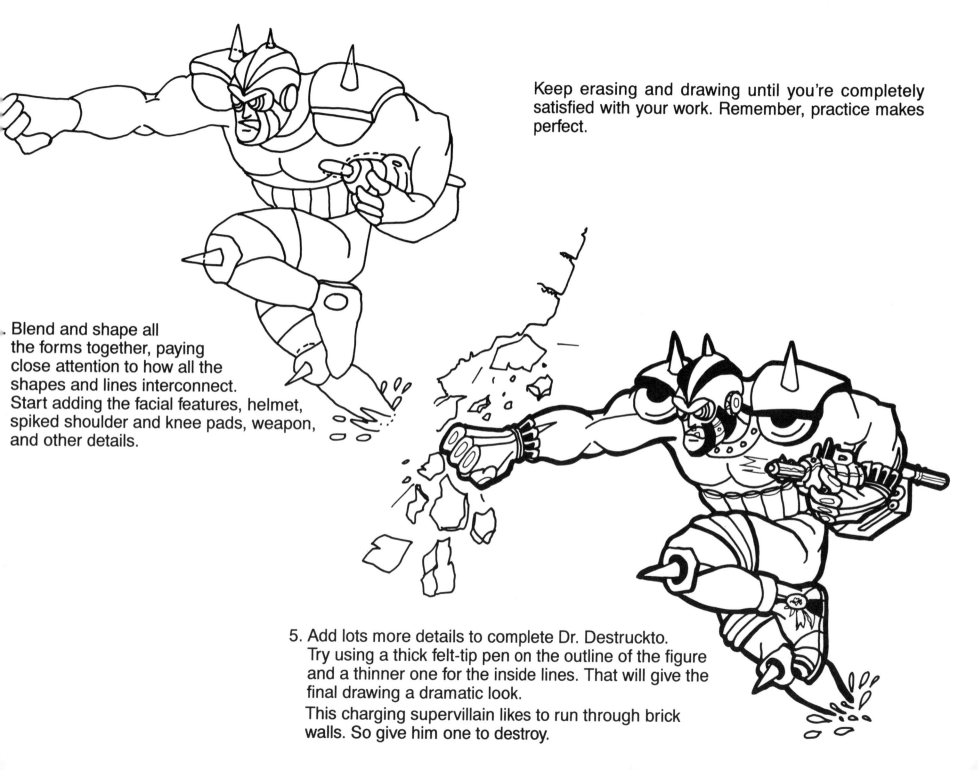

Keep erasing and drawing until you're completely satisfied with your work. Remember, practice makes perfect.

Blend and shape all the forms together, paying close attention to how all the shapes and lines interconnect. Start adding the facial features, helmet, spiked shoulder and knee pads, weapon, and other details.

5. Add lots more details to complete Dr. Destruckto. Try using a thick felt-tip pen on the outline of the figure and a thinner one for the inside lines. That will give the final drawing a dramatic look.

This charging supervillain likes to run through brick walls. So give him one to destroy.

WAYNE, THE WICKED PIRATE

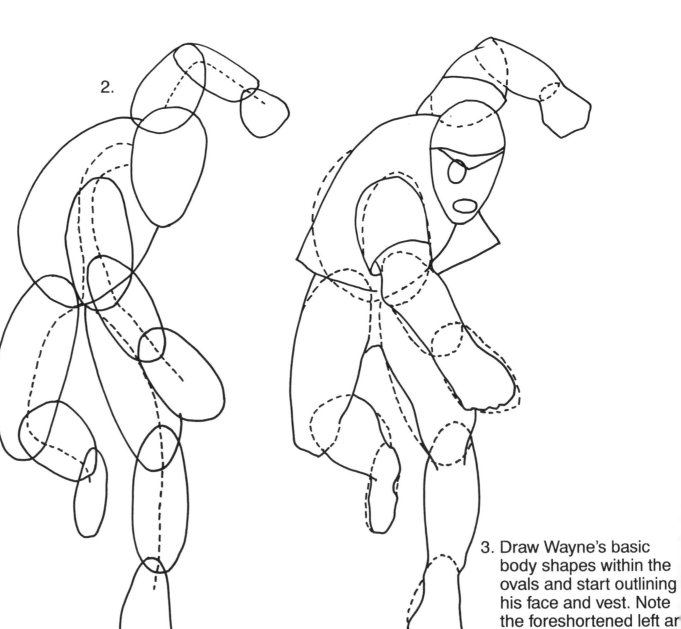

1.

2.

1.& 2. Draw the flowing lines of the stick figure and add the oval body shapes. Be careful. There are lots of large overlapping shapes here.

Pay special attention to the overlapping ovals on the right leg. The right calf is much shorter than the left calf. This is another example of foreshortening. Your eyes are fooled and don't see the full length of the leg. Draw it the way it **looks** and not how it really is.

3. Draw Wayne's basic body shapes within the ovals and start outlining his face and vest. Note the foreshortened left ar

4. Erase unnecessary guidelines as you blend the shapes together and curve all the body lines. Start defining the facial features, boots, and clothes. Add the sword, wrist bracelets, and the bandanna on his head.

5. Add the finishing touches to this supervillain by completing all the details. Pointed teeth give him a menacing look. When you're done, add some colors to this wicked pirate.

SHE-HAWK

1.

1. & 2. Draw the line figures for the two figures in the poses as shown. Then, add the various body shapes. Note how the bird's shape differs from the human one.

2.

3. Add the hawk's wing and tail guidelines and begin sketching in its feet and beak. Start forming She-Hawk's body by combining the oval guidelines, erasing the stick figure as you go along.

Make sure you have built a solid foundation with the first two steps before continuing.

4. Blend She-Hawk's body shapes together and add the face, hair, and clothes. Complete the bird's head, legs, and feet. Feathers are fun to draw. Do them a row at a time, letting them overlap a little.

If you're not satisfied with the way any part of your drawing looks, erase it and start again.

5. Finish this supervillain's clothes and face, and add all the final details to her and the hawk so they may fly off to seek trouble.

SLIME-O

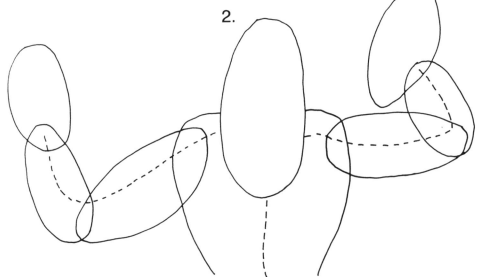

1. & 2. Starting with a large oval, draw the simple stick figure. Then, add the shapes for the arms, hands, and chest.

3. Start outlining the various parts of the head and face, adding muck and slime to the lower part of the face. Begin forming the arm sections and clawed hands. Once you've completed this part of the figure, you're ready for the fun part.

Remember to keep all your guidelines lightly drawn.

4. Finish the claws and continue to add details to the face and head. This supervillain spends lots of time underwater, so draw scales on his arms and body. He's also covered with seaweed as he comes crashing out of the water.

5. Continue adding details to Slime-o, making him as yucky-mucky as you wish. This is a good place to use your imagination. What do you think his mouth and teeth, or the rest of his body, looks like?

KAPTAIN KRYPTO

1.

1. & 2. Lightly draw the stick figure and all the guide-line shapes around it. It's a little more compli-cated when you have two overlapping figures, but if you're extra careful and follow along step by step, you'll soon have a fine finished drawing.

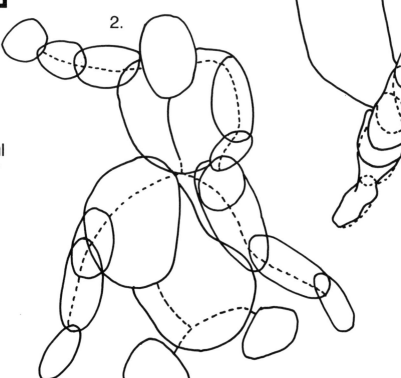

2.

3. First, sketch the body parts within the oval shapes, paying careful attention to the way the two figures interact. Next, draw the basic outlines of the two heads. Then, add guideline shapes for the cape, wings and tail.

Remember to erase any unnecessary lines as you continue to refine your drawing.

Note: **Don't** continue unless you are satisfied with the way your drawing looks at this stage.

5. Continue to refine your drawing as you add all the details that place this twosome among the most feared supervillains of all time.

4. Do the human figure first. Complete the face, hands, arms, legs, and boots. Add the lance. Then start working on the dragon. Sketch in the teeth and claws and begin adding scales to the body. Define the dragon's wings and tail. Don't forget to add the row of horns on his head.

Here's an example of what a supervillain's city might look like.
Use your imagination and create a few of your own.

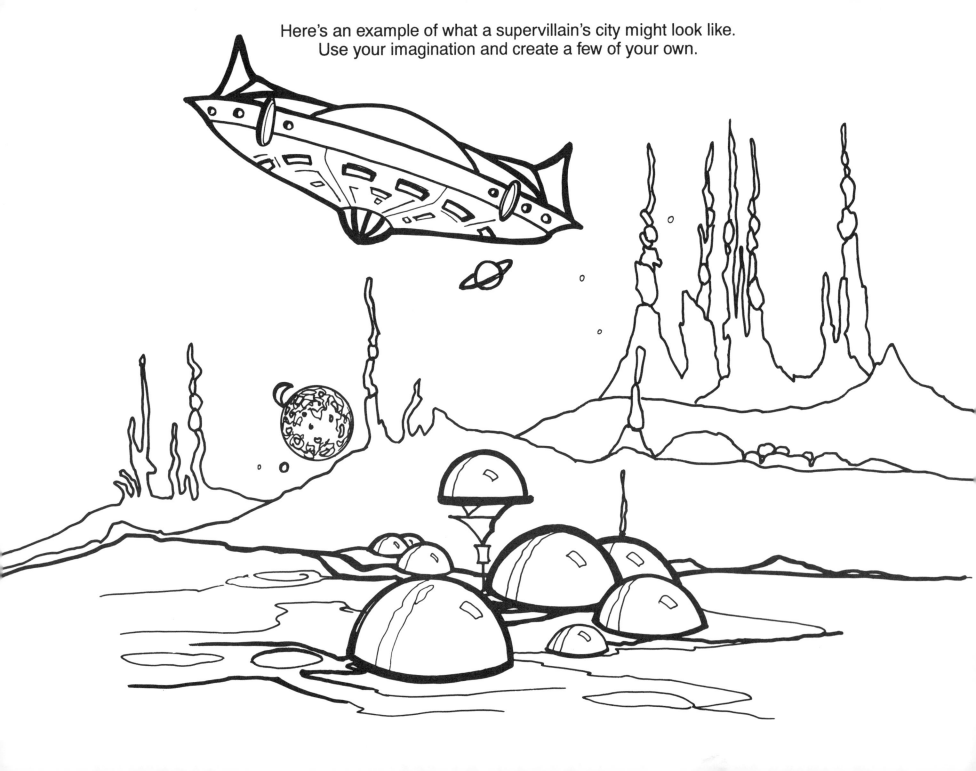

HOW TO DRAW
MORE SUPERHEROES

Illustrated by Jael

DEFENDRO

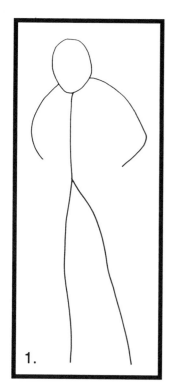

1.

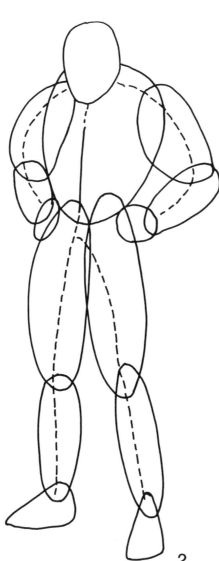

2.

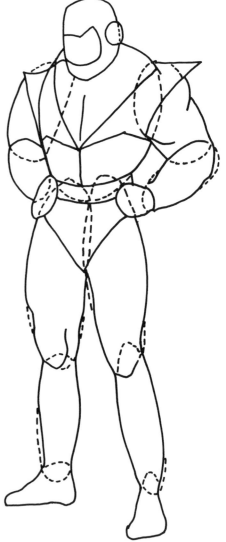

1. & 2. Starting with the head, draw the simple stick figure (gesture lines). Then add the other ovals and guideline shapes.

Note: Keep all your guidelines lightly drawn. They will be easier to erase later on.

3. Start defining and shaping the arms, fingers, legs, and torso within the oval guidelines, erasing your gesture lines as you go along. Begin outlining this superhero's helmet and uniform.

4. Add the facial features and complete the helmet and clothing. Erase any guidelines you no longer need as you begin to add details.

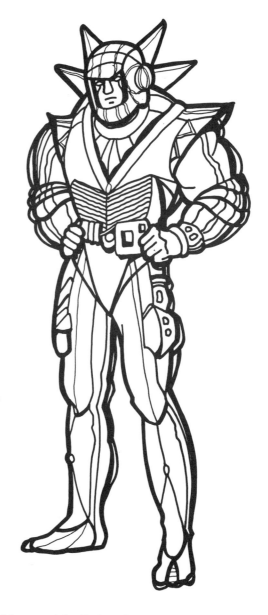

Before going to the next step, make sure that you are satisfied with the way your drawing looks so far.

5. Now add all the finishing touches and final details, and Defendro is ready for defensive action!

GORY THE GLADIATOR

Note: Step #3 is a very important step. It establishes the basic overall structure and look of your drawing. In steps 4 and 5 you are simply refining and adding details to the figure you have created in step 3.

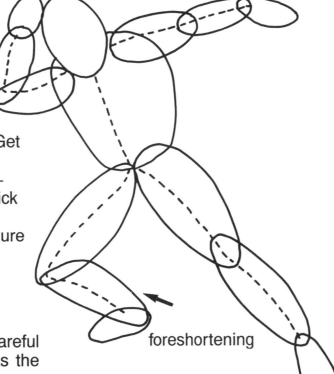

1. & 2. Begin by lightly drawing the basic line figure. Then add the overlapping ovals and other guideline body shapes.

Note: Draw these key steps carefully. Get the stick figure to gesture in the directions you want it to. By carefully adding the ovals over the stick figure, you have created a solid foundation. This will give your figure a more realistic look after you've completed the next steps.

Note foreshortening here. Be careful not to make this calf as long as the other one.

foreshortening

2.

3. Start defining the muscles within the oval guidelines and add guideline shapes for Gory the Gladiator's cape, clothes, and headgear. Erase any unnecessary guidelines.

4. Blend the body shapes together as you continue adding the clothes. Outline the cape and skirted part of the tunic; add the facial details, sword, and fingers.

5. Complete your superhero by adding lots of details to his outfit. When you're finished, add some hot colors for dramatic effect.

THE MIGHTY POWER PACKER

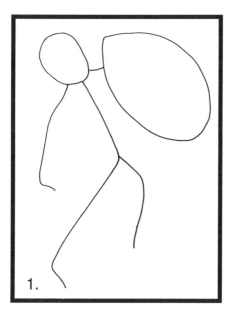

1.

Remember: It's easy to draw almost anything if you first build a good foundation.

1. & 2. Begin this superhero with the lightly drawn stick figure and his power shield. Then draw the oval guidelines for the body and the outline of his power-packed weapon.

2.

3. Define the body sections within the oval outlines, erasing the stick figure and other guidelines you no longer need. Add guidelines for the fingers, clothes, and headgear, and start adding details to the weapon.

Note: If you're not satisfied with any part of your drawing, erase it and start again.

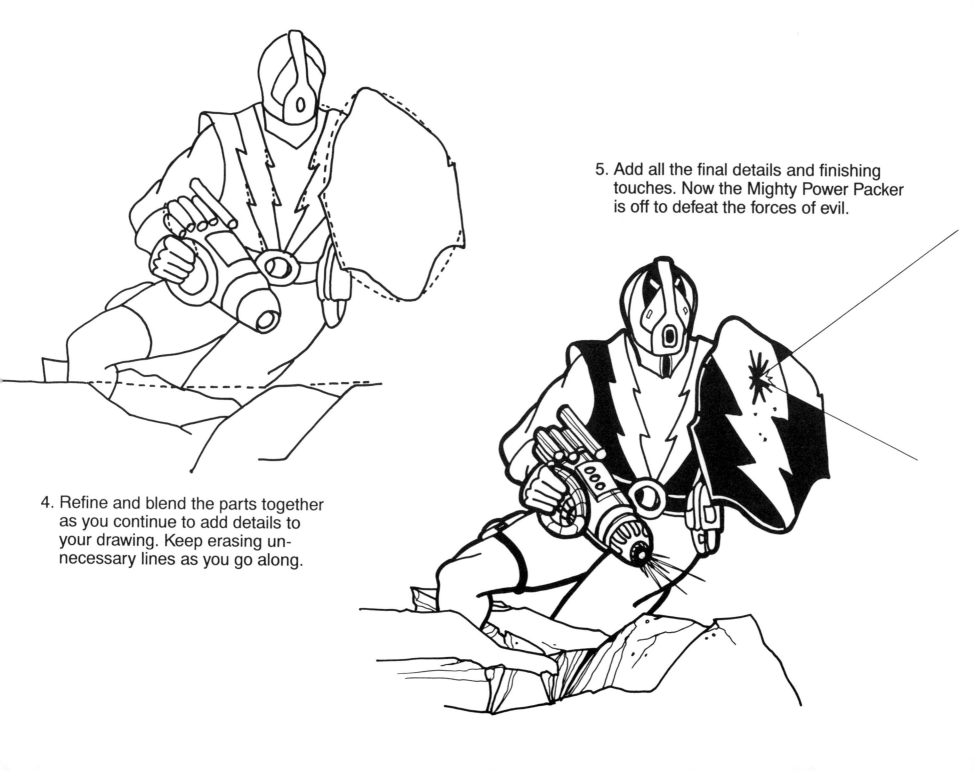

5. Add all the final details and finishing touches. Now the Mighty Power Packer is off to defeat the forces of evil.

4. Refine and blend the parts together as you continue to add details to your drawing. Keep erasing unnecessary lines as you go along.

PRINCESS SWORD

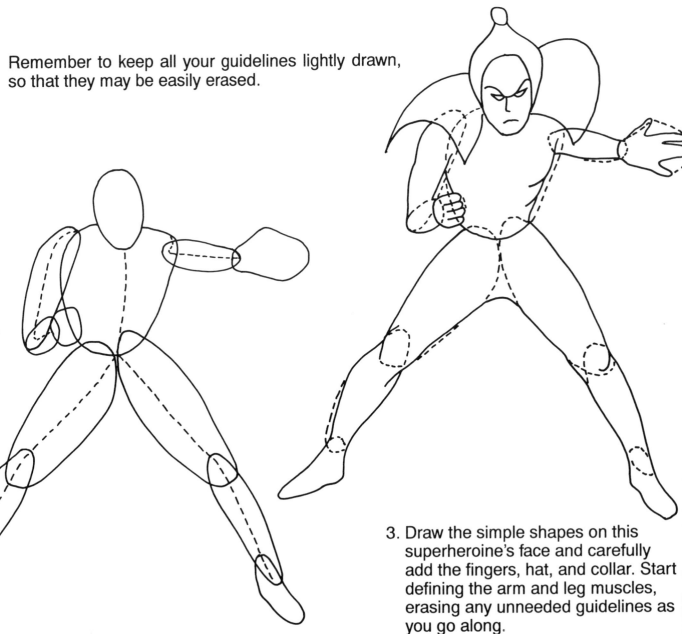

Remember to keep all your guidelines lightly drawn, so that they may be easily erased.

1.

1. & 2. Starting with the head, draw the gesture lines. Then add the guideline shapes for the arms, legs, and torso.

2.

3. Draw the simple shapes on this superheroine's face and carefully add the fingers, hat, and collar. Start defining the arm and leg muscles, erasing any unneeded guidelines as you go along.

4. Complete the facial features, hands, and fingers. Blend the parts together and add the clothes and sword. Then begin adding details as shown.

Keep erasing and drawing until you are satisfied with your drawing.

5. Now you're ready to add lots of details and final touches to your drawing of Princess Sword. Don't forget the pointy fingernails and the plume on her hat.

REFLECTRON

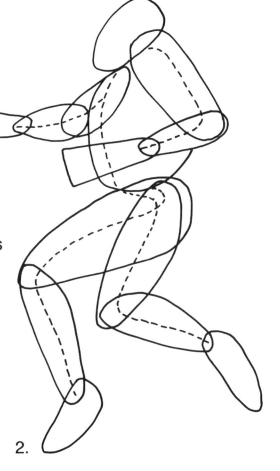

1.

1. & 2. Draw the basic stick figure and all the overlapping, oval body guidelines. Note that the ovals are different shapes and sizes. (The hand shapes are not ovals). Draw them carefully. This will make it easier to draw the muscle shapes within them.

2.

3. Define the body shapes within the oval guidelines, as you carefully erase the stick figure and other unnecessary guide lines.

4. Blend and smooth all the shapes together. Add clothing and the reflectors on his knees, belt, elbow, shoulder, and head. Since the figure is looking away, only a small profile of the face can be seen.

Lightly draw reflection lines fanning out from the reflectors. Then go over them with a ruler to make them straight and strong.

5. Complete this superhero by adding more defining body lines and all the details.

AQUATO THE ADVENTUROUS

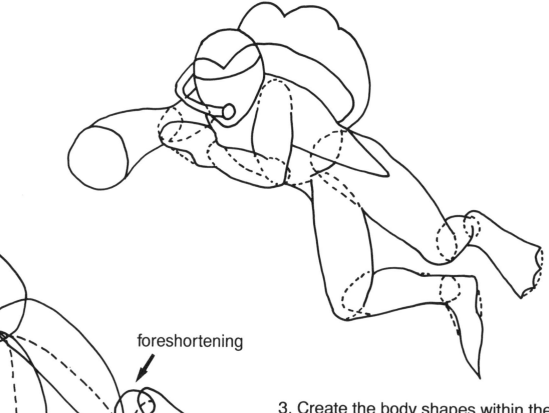

1. & 2. Draw the line figure and the oval body shapes around them. Note the guideline shapes for Aquato's feet.

2.

Note foreshortening as his left calf is pointing away from the viewer.

foreshortening

Note: Make sure your figure is gesturing in the direction you want it to before continuing to step 3.

3. Create the body shapes within the ovals and add additional guidelines for the underwater helmet, air tanks, and weapon. Begin forming the hand and body suit.

Erase any guidelines you no longer need.

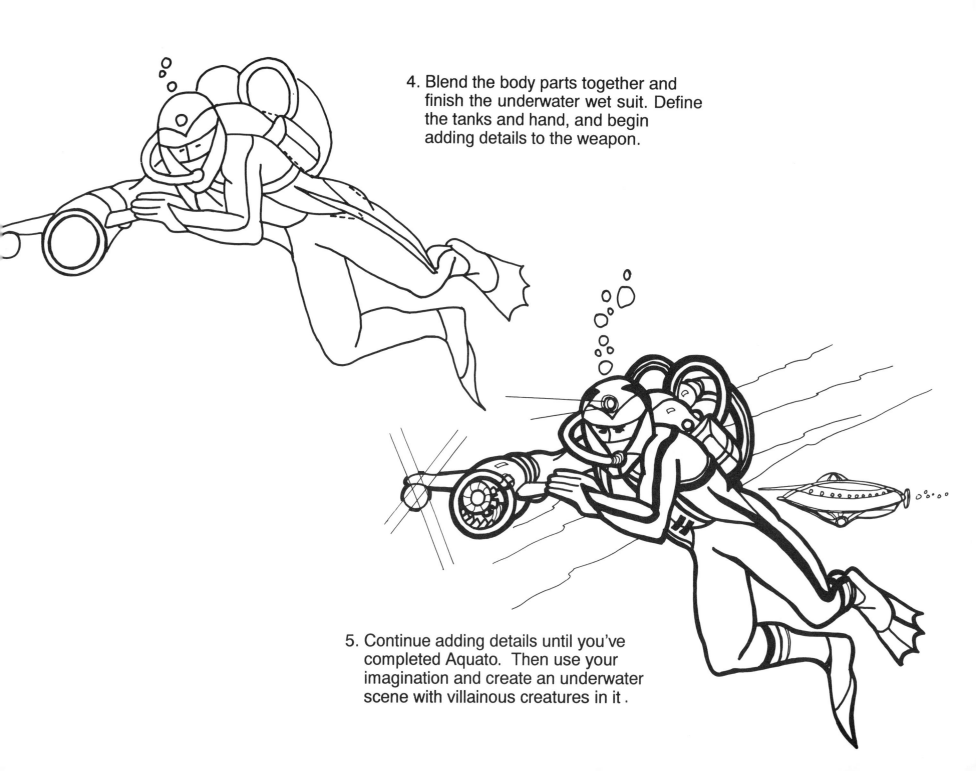

4. Blend the body parts together and finish the underwater wet suit. Define the tanks and hand, and begin adding details to the weapon.

5. Continue adding details until you've completed Aquato. Then use your imagination and create an underwater scene with villainous creatures in it .

Superheroes and superheroines often have buddies, or sidekicks, who help them in their quests.
Try to draw these few examples, adding them to your drawings.
Then create your own characters.

Here are a few more "sidekicks" to add to your drawings.

FALCONER

1.

2.

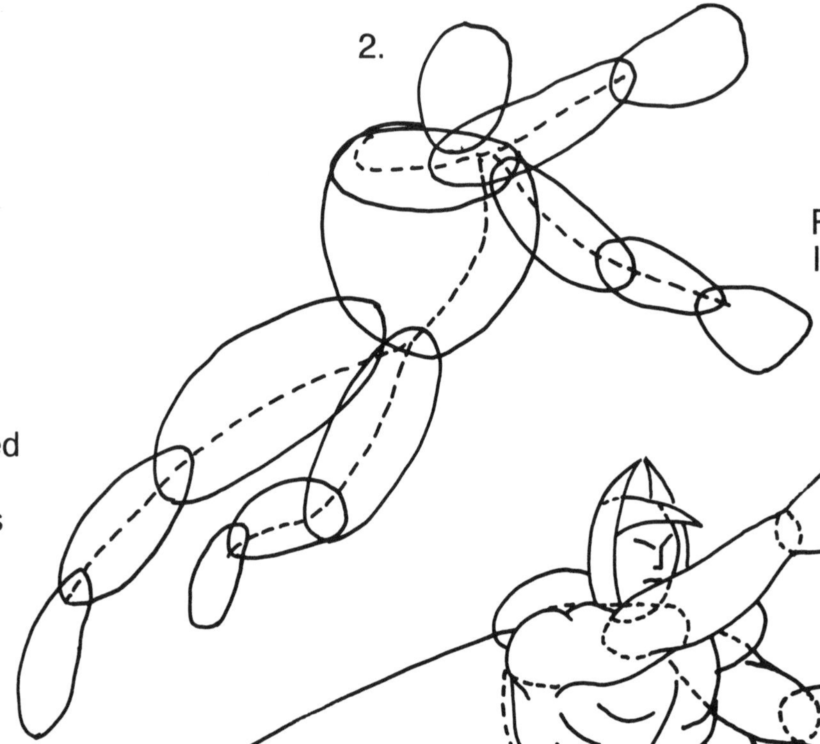

Remember to keep these guidelines lightly drawn.

1. & 2. Starting with the oval-shaped head, draw the stick figure. Add the broad body shapes for the muscular arms, legs, and chest.

Note: Superheroes usually have exaggerated muscle lines that make them appear powerful and strong.

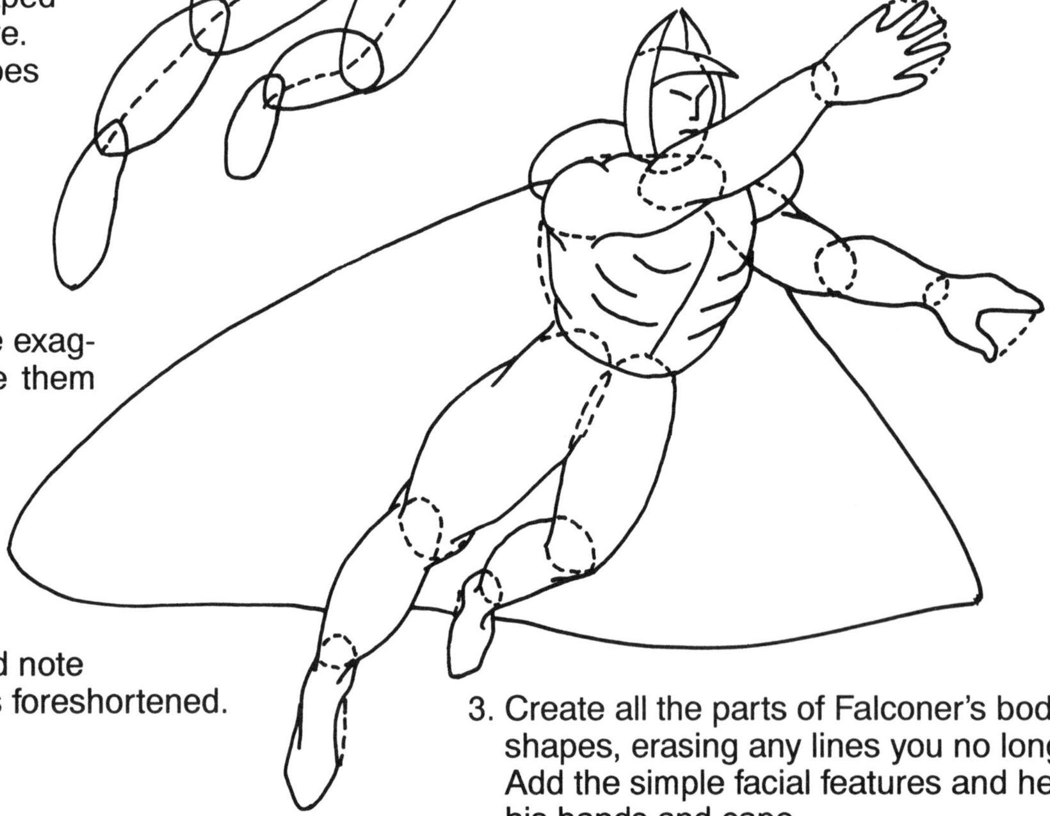

As this superhero lunges forward note how his left leg, pointing away, is foreshortened.

3. Create all the parts of Falconer's body within the guideline shapes, erasing any lines you no longer need as you go alon Add the simple facial features and helmet, and guidelines for his hands and cape.

5. Add the additional body lines and all the finishing touches, as shown. Remember to use your imagination when adding details. Draw a different uniform; add a weapon; a mask.

4. Begin blending the body parts together. Outline the cape and start adding the outfit and accessories. Note how the thickness of the muscles makes the superhero look powerful.

Keep sketching and erasing until you are satisfied with your work.

KIT THE COURAGEOUS

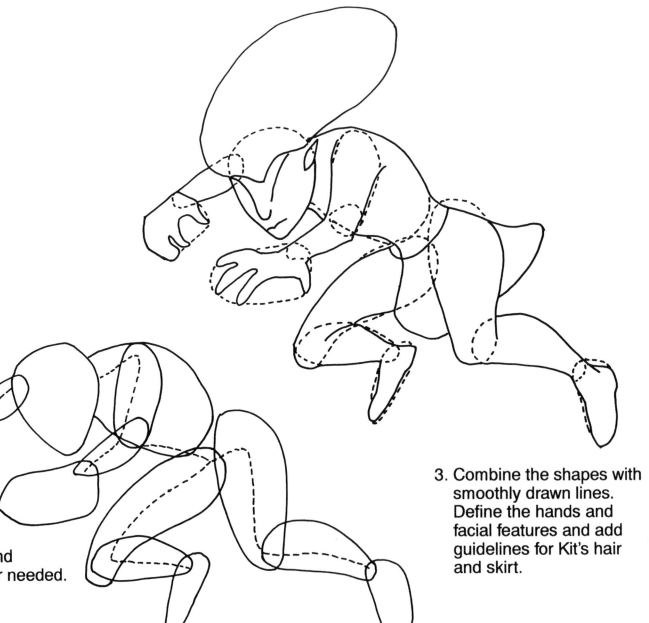

1.

1. & 2. After creating the basic
stick figure, add the
guideline body shapes.
Note that the right arm
looks short because
part of it is hidden behind
the head. Stand in front of
a mirror and try this pose.

2.

Remember to erase the stick figure and
the other guidelines that are no longer needed.

3. Combine the shapes with
smoothly drawn lines.
Define the hands and
facial features and add
guidelines for Kit's hair
and skirt.

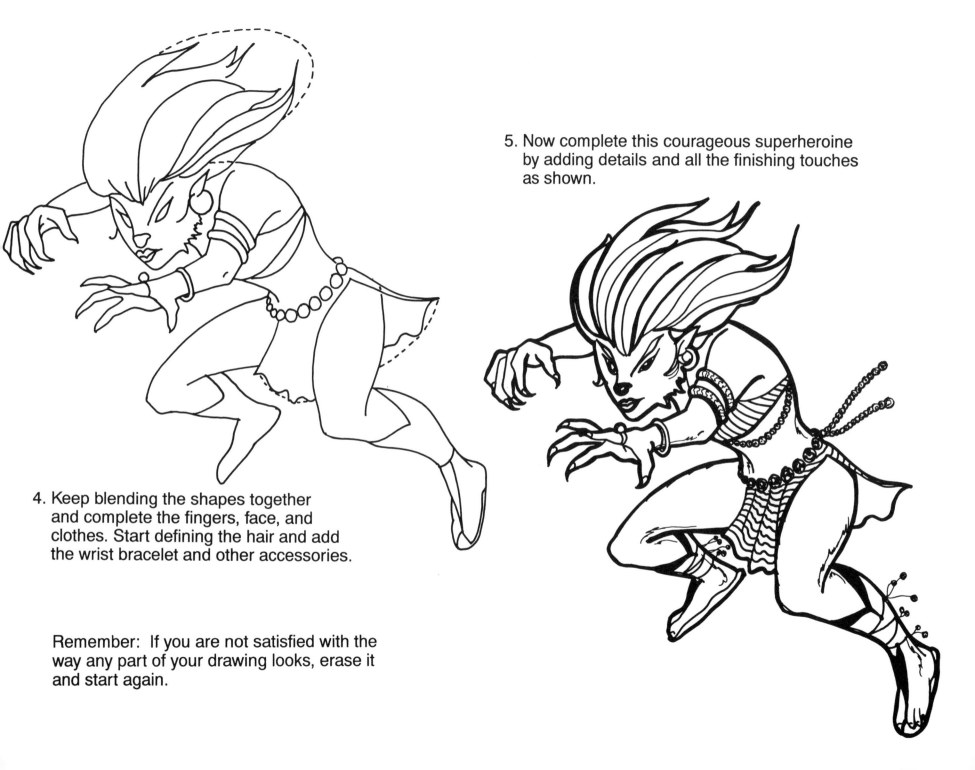

4. Keep blending the shapes together and complete the fingers, face, and clothes. Start defining the hair and add the wrist bracelet and other accessories.

Remember: If you are not satisfied with the way any part of your drawing looks, erase it and start again.

5. Now complete this courageous superheroine by adding details and all the finishing touches as shown.

POWER PUNCHER

1.

1. & 2. Lightly draw the gesturing stick figure and all the overlapping guideline shapes around it.

foreshortening

2.

3. Within the ovals, create the muscular legs and outline the clothing on his upper body. Keep erasing the stick figure guideline as you go along. Start defining the left hand and the power pack on the right one.

Use foreshortening when any part of the body points away from you, the viewer. This gives your figure a dramatic, 3-dimensional look.

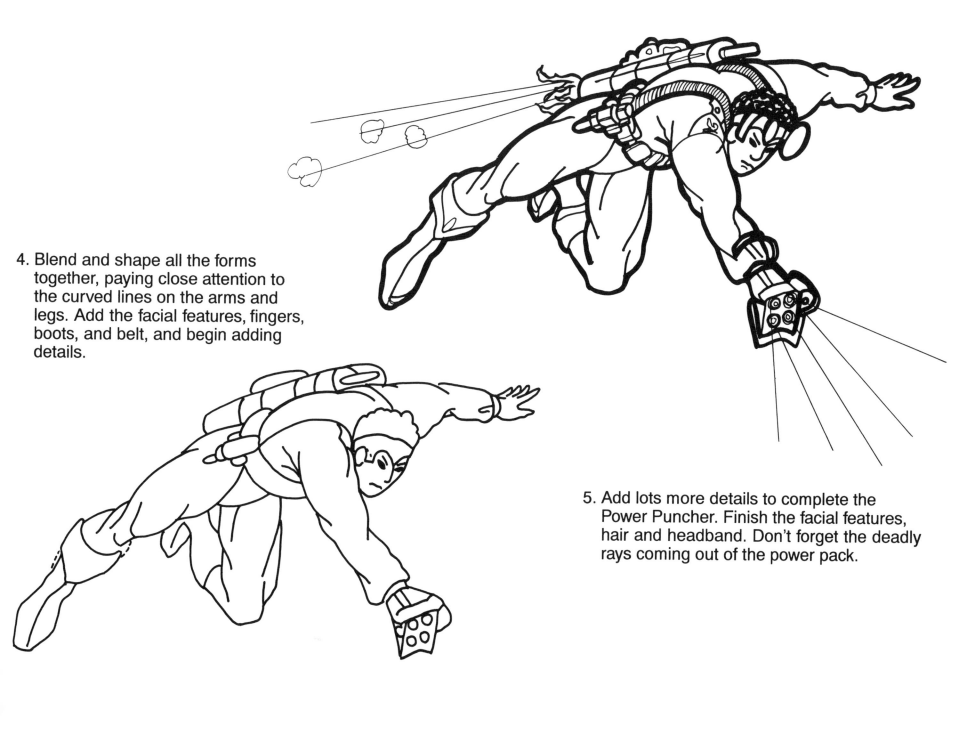

4. Blend and shape all the forms together, paying close attention to the curved lines on the arms and legs. Add the facial features, fingers, boots, and belt, and begin adding details.

5. Add lots more details to complete the Power Puncher. Finish the facial features, hair and headband. Don't forget the deadly rays coming out of the power pack.

SKY GLIDER

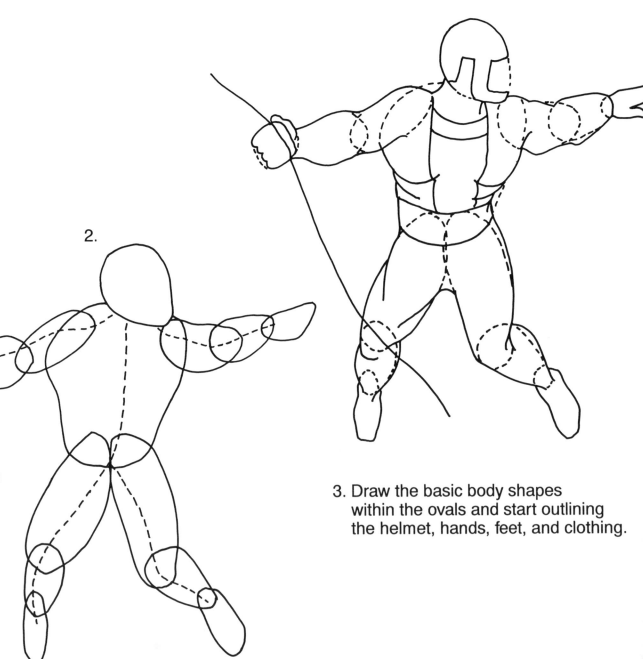

1. & 2. Make sure the legs of the guideline stick figure are spread far enough apart to allow for the powerful leg muscles. Then add the large oval body shapes. Note the huge chest on this superhero.

Remember to keep all your guidelines lightly drawn.

2.

3. Draw the basic body shapes within the ovals and start outlining the helmet, hands, feet, and clothing.

5. Add the finishing touches to Sky Glider by completing all the details. And make sure you've given him something to hang on to. When you're done, give your drawing a dramatic look by outlining it with a heavy felt-tip pen.

4. Erase unnecessary guidelines as you blend the shapes together. Carefully curve the body lines as you begin adding details to the face and uniform.

OLYMPIA

If you're not satisfied with the way any part of your drawing looks, erase it and start again.

1. & 2. Draw the simple line figure in the action pose as shown. Then, add the various overlapping oval shapes.

Make sure you have built a solid foundation with the first two steps before continuing.

1.

2.

3. Sketch the body parts within the oval guidelines, erasing as you go along. Begin forming Olympia's hands, hair, and outfit. Then use a ruler to draw the long, straight spear.

4. Blend the body shapes together and complete the hands and face. Continue drawing Olympia's flowing hair and add her boots and bracelets.

5. Complete this superheroine by finishing her hair and adding details to her boots and outfit.

THE VAPOR RANGER

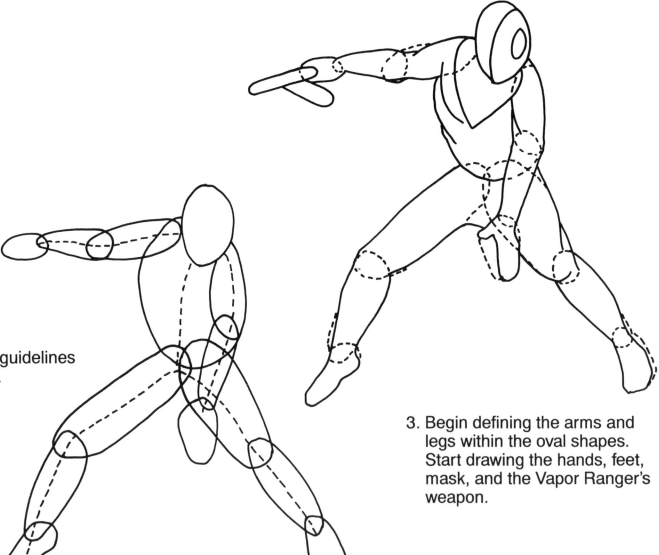

1.

1. & 2. Starting with the head, draw the simple stick figure. Then lightly sketch all the basic guideline body shapes.

Remember to erase any unnecessary guidelines as you continue to refine your drawing.

2.

3. Begin defining the arms and legs within the oval shapes. Start drawing the hands, feet, mask, and the Vapor Ranger's weapon.

4. Blend the shapes into a smooth body outline. Then, add the uniform, including the
face mask, and vapor sources on the shoulders
and legs. Complete the hands, feet, and weapon,
and start adding puffs of vapor.

When you're finished, use a thick marker to
outline the Vapor Ranger. This gives your picture
a more dramatic look.

5. Continue adding details to the uniform as you
continue to refine your drawing. Keep erasing
and sketching until you're satisfied with the
way your superhero looks.

KNIGHT-MARE

Two overlapping figures are more difficult to draw. Just follow along carefully, step by step, and you'll soon have a fine finished drawing.

1.

1. & 2. Lightly draw the stick figures for the knight and horse and all the guideline shapes around them.

2.

Remember to erase any lines you no longer need as you go along.

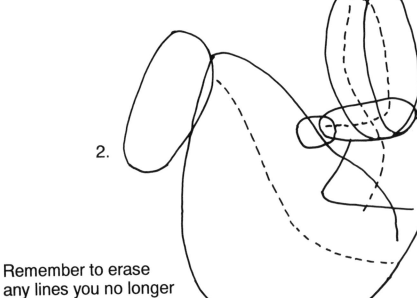

3. First, lightly sketch the features on the horse's head, as shown. Then, shape the knight's head and body within the guidelines. Lastly, add a large guideline shape for the knight's flowing cape.

5. Add all the remaining details. Use your imagination and add an interesting background. When you're finished, add your favorite colors for the final touch.

4. Keep blending and refining the shapes into a smooth, continuous form. Starting with the horse, complete the facial features, mane, and reins. Then draw in the knight's face and helmet, and carefully begin adding details to his clothing. Create his cape and add the sword and helmet plume.

Add the finishing touches **after** you are satisfied with the way Knight-Mare looks.

Here's another example of a futuristic city and a few spacecraft. Try drawing these, then use your imagination to create others. Adding a background to your drawing gives it a "finished" look.

HOW TO DRAW MORE SUPERVILLAINS

Illustrated by **Jael**

THE VAPORIZER

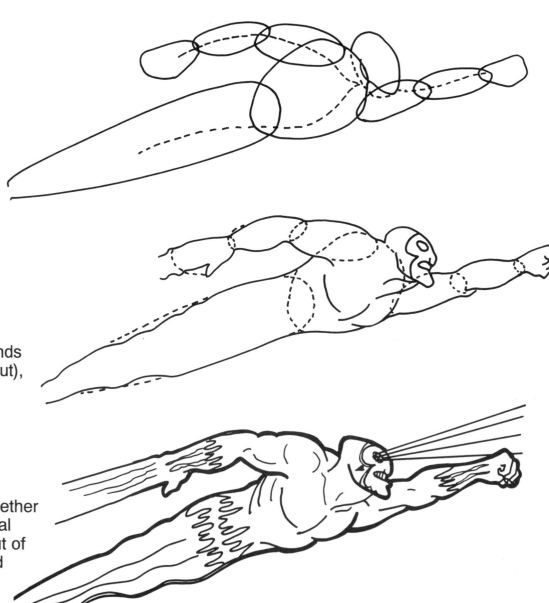

1.& 2. Draw the basic stick figure and all the overlapping oval body guidelines.

Make sure you have built a solid foundation with the first two steps before continuing.

3. Sketch the body parts within the oval guidelines. Begin forming the Vaporizer's hands and facial features (note how his chin juts out), erasing guidelines as you go along.

4. Blend the arm, shoulder, and chest muscles together into a smooth upper body shape. Finish the facial features and add the vaporizing lines coming out of his eye. Extend the flowing body and right-hand lines, and add the final details.

THE MEANY GENIE

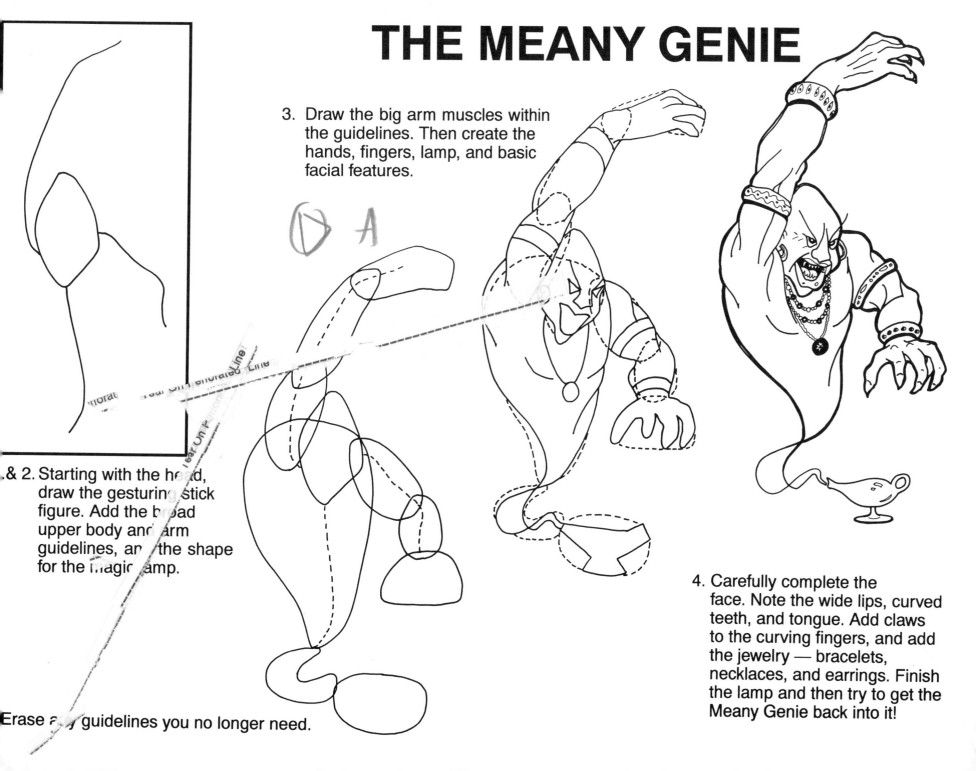

3. Draw the big arm muscles within the guidelines. Then create the hands, fingers, lamp, and basic facial features.

& 2. Starting with the head, draw the gesturing stick figure. Add the broad upper body and arm guidelines, and the shape for the magic lamp.

Erase any guidelines you no longer need.

4. Carefully complete the face. Note the wide lips, curved teeth, and tongue. Add claws to the curving fingers, and add the jewelry — bracelets, necklaces, and earrings. Finish the lamp and then try to get the Meany Genie back into it!

DARK DEMON

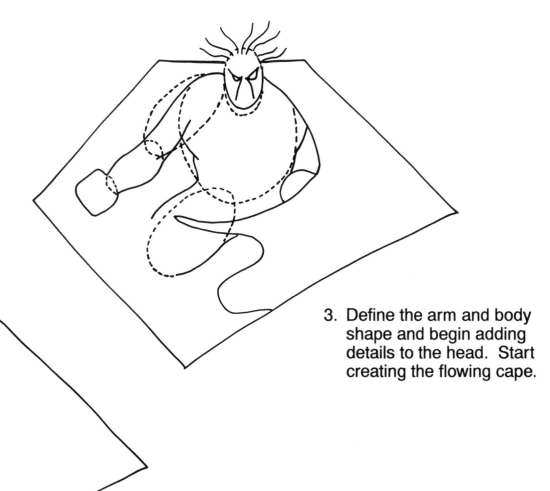

1.& 2. Begin by lightly drawing the basic line figure. Then add the ovals for the body parts and the surrounding straight lines for the cape.

3. Define the arm and body shape and begin adding details to the head. Start creating the flowing cape.

It's easy to draw almost anything if you first build a good foundation.

4. Draw the fingers and blend the body shapes together as you add the clothes. Add the rest of the facial features and complete the cape's outline. Begin adding details.

5. Add all the final details and shading to his face, hair, and clothes. Use a felt-tip pen to complete this super-villain. A heavy outline always adds a dramatic effect to your drawing. Don't forget to attach the arrowheads.

Note: Since most villains are sourpusses, their mouths curve downwards.

GRETA, THE GHASTLY GIANT

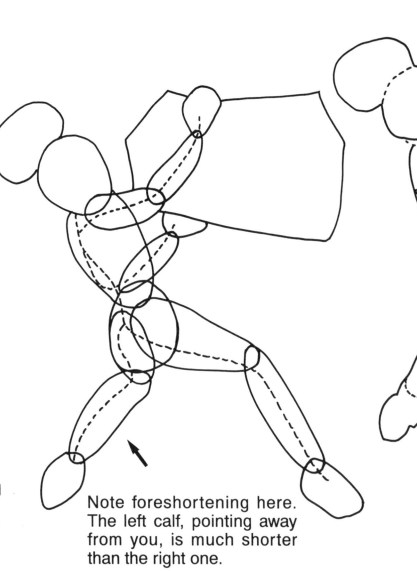

1. & 2. Begin this supervillain with the lightly drawn stick figure. Then draw the oval guidelines for the body outline and the outline of the house.

Note: Draw these key steps carefully. Get the stick figure to gesture in the directions you want it to. By carefully adding the ovals over the stick figure, you have created a solid foundation. This will give your figure a more realistic look after you've completed the next steps.

Note foreshortening here. The left calf, pointing away from you, is much shorter than the right one.

3. Define the body sections within the oval outlines, erasing the stick figure and other guidelines you no longer need.

Add guidelines for her vest and begin shaping the house.

5. Add all the final details and finishing touches as shown. Now Greta can complete her super-villainous mission.

4. Curve and blend all the parts together into a smooth body shape. Add guidelines for the boots, ball and chain, and clothes.

Continue adding wrecking lines to the house.

Note: If you're not satisfied with any part of your drawing, erase and start again.

TORMENT-O-RATOR

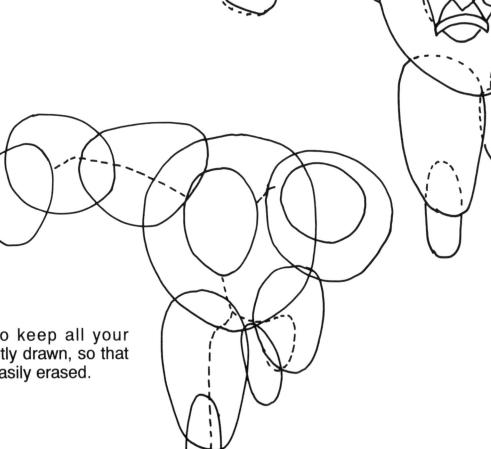

1.& 2. Draw the oval for the
head and the gesture
lines. Then add all the
overlapping ovals for
the arms, legs, and torso.

Remember to keep all your
guidelines lightly drawn, so that
they may be easily erased.

3. Draw the simple
shapes on Torment-o-
Rator's face and care-
fully add the fingers.
Define the arm and leg
sections, erasing any
unnecessary guide-
lines as you go along.

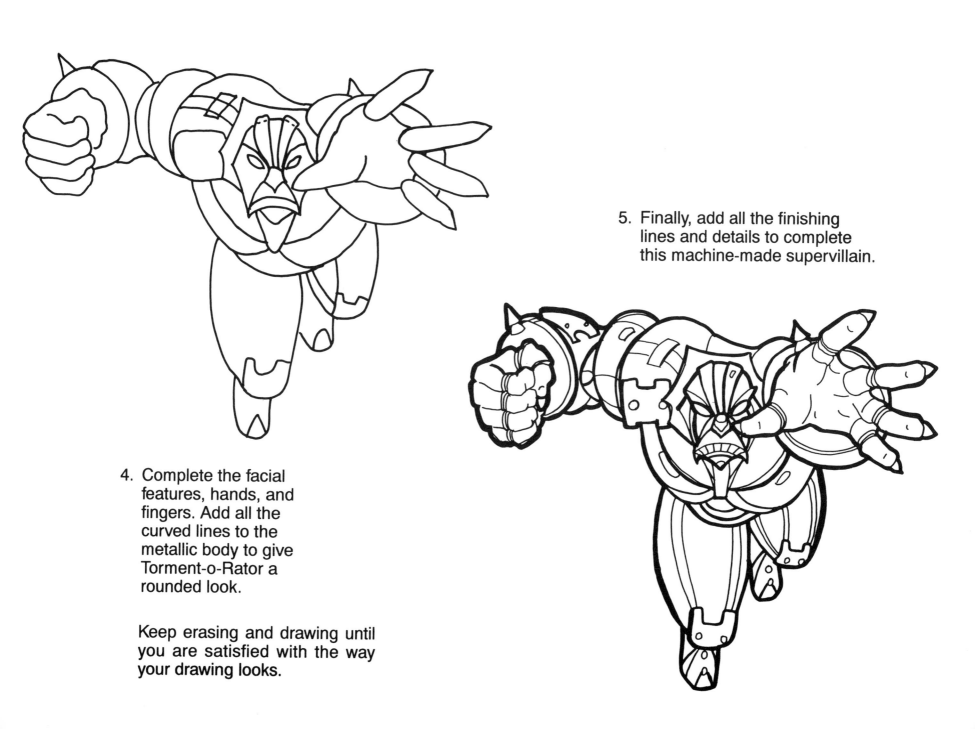

5. Finally, add all the finishing lines and details to complete this machine-made supervillain.

4. Complete the facial features, hands, and fingers. Add all the curved lines to the metallic body to give Torment-o-Rator a rounded look.

Keep erasing and drawing until you are satisfied with the way your drawing looks.

LITTLE LIONEL

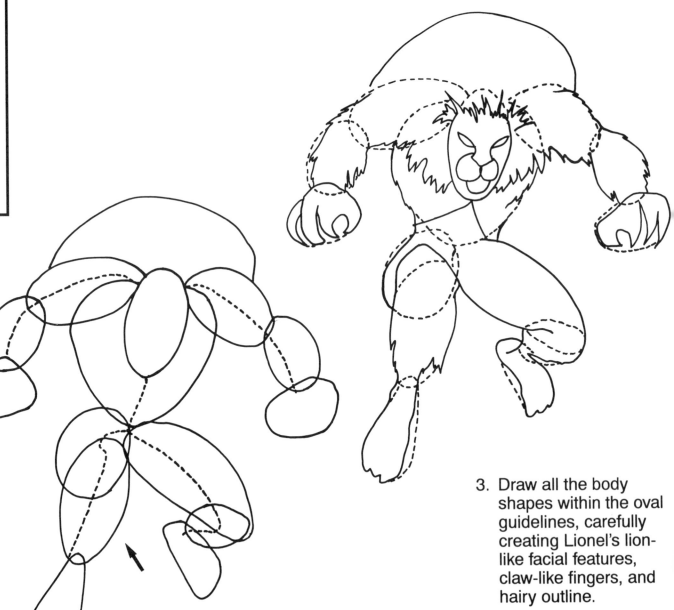

1.& 2. Draw the basic stick figure and all the oval body guidelines. Note that the ovals are different shapes and sizes. Draw them carefully. This will make it easier to draw the muscle shapes within them.

Erase the stick figure and other unnecessary guidelines as you go along.

Foreshorten

3. Draw all the body shapes within the oval guidelines, carefully creating Lionel's lion-like facial features, claw-like fingers, and hairy outline.

5. Complete Little Lionel by adding fangs and claws, and all the other details.

4. Blend and smooth all the shapes together. Add the bushy mane and finish shaping the face.

THE PIT BULLY

1.& 2. Draw the standing line figure and the oval guideline body shapes. Add guidelines for the cape.

Make sure your figure is gesturing in the direction you want it to before continuing to step 3.

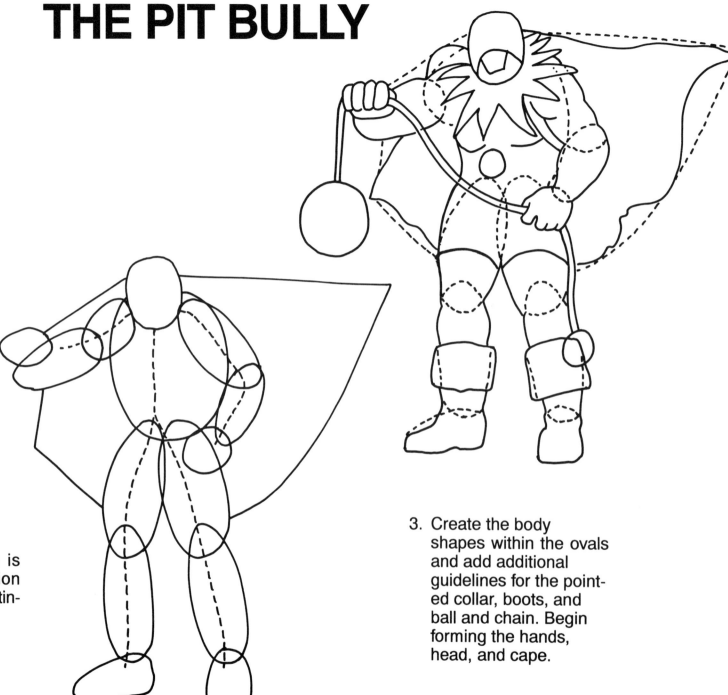

3. Create the body shapes within the ovals and add additional guidelines for the pointed collar, boots, and ball and chain. Begin forming the hands, head, and cape.

4. Blend Pit Bully's body parts together and finish drawing his hands. Begin adding details to the clothes, head, and ball and chain. Complete the cape.

Erase any guidelines you no longer need and when you're satisfied with the way your drawing looks, start adding the finishing touches.

5. Add all the final details and shading to complete this supervillain. Now your personal Pit Bully is ready for some hair-raising havoc!

Note: Supervillains have abnormally large muscle lines that make them appear powerful and dangerous.

BUSTER THE BAD

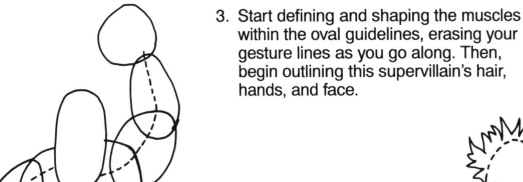

3. Start defining and shaping the muscles within the oval guidelines, erasing your gesture lines as you go along. Then, begin outlining this supervillain's hair, hands, and face.

1.& 2. Starting with the head, draw the simple stick figure (gesture lines). Then add the various overlapping ovals and other guideline shapes.

Use foreshortening when any part of the body points away from you, the viewer. This gives your figure a dramatic, 3-dimensional look.

Note: Keep all your guidelines lightly drawn. They will be easier to erase later on.

4. Complete the hair and facial features. Sharply define the hands, and Buster's arm and leg muscles. Then, begin adding the rings on his limbs and other details.

Any unnecessary guidelines should be erased before going to step #5.

5. Now add all the final details and finishing touches, and Buster is ready to be bad!

RATSY RIZZI

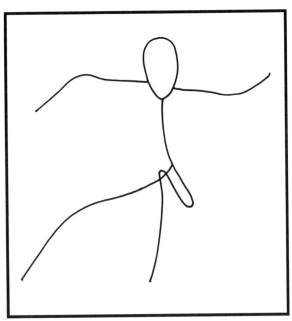

1.& 2. Starting with the oval-shaped head, draw the basic stick figure. Add the broad body ovals and shapes for the hands, feet, and ears.

3. Create all the parts of Ratsy's body within the guideline shapes. Add guidelines for her facial features, mask, and gloves.

Pay special attention to the overlapping ovals on the upper left leg. This is another example of foreshortening. Your eyes are fooled and don't see the full length of the leg. Draw it the way it **looks** and not how it really is. Remember to keep these guidelines lightly drawn.

4. Finish the facial features, mask, and gloves. Begin adding the tail. Blend all the shapes into a smooth outline, erasing any lines you no longer need as you go along.

5. Complete the tail and add all the finishing touches. Don't forget Ratsy's whiskers. Use your imagination when adding details. Draw a different mask or clothes if you wish. Or, create a scene with several supervillains in it.

GRAFFITI GUS

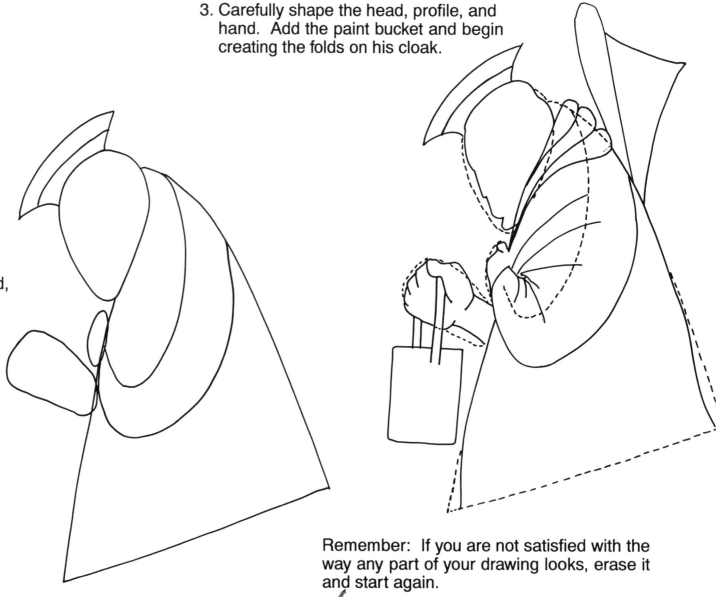

3. Carefully shape the head, profile, and hand. Add the paint bucket and begin creating the folds on his cloak.

1.& 2. Starting with a large oval shape for the head, create the basic figure, drawing the additional shapes as shown.

Remember: If you are not satisfied with the way any part of your drawing looks, erase it and start again.

Erase any guidelines that are no longer needed.

5. Now complete your drawing by adding lots of details and shading. For the finishing touches, add some of Gus's favorite graffiti.

4. Finish the face and hair, and add the brushes and dripping paint. Complete the supervillain's flowing cloak.

MAGNET-O-MAN

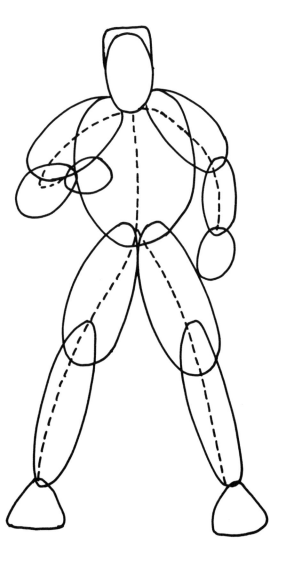

1. & 2. Lightly draw the standing stick figure and all the oval guideline shapes around it.

3. Within the ovals, create the basic body parts, erasing the stick figure as you go along. Carefully add guidelines for his magnetized chest shield, belt, and knee guards.

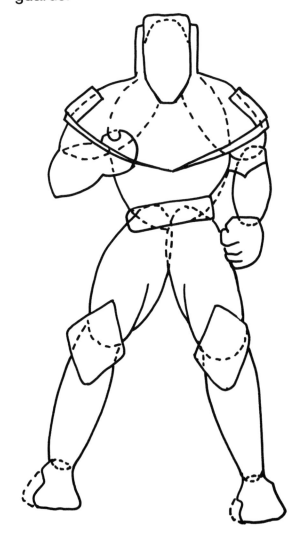

4. Blend and shape all the forms together, paying close attention to how all the shapes and lines interconnect. Start adding the facial features, hood, boots, magneto spear, and other details.

Keep erasing and drawing until you're completely satisfied with your work. Remember, practice makes perfect.

5. Add lots more details to complete Magnet-O-Man. Note how the use of heavy lines gives the final drawing a dramatic look.

HULKOID, THE WILD BIKER

Remember to keep all your guidelines lightly drawn.

1.& 2. Make sure the legs of the guideline stick figure are spread far apart to allow for the powerful leg muscles and bike. Then add the large oval shapes for the body and tire.

3. Draw the basic body shapes within the ovals and start outlining the face, helmet, fingers, and boots. Note the foreshortened arms. Add the handlebars and other parts of the bike.

5. Add the finishing touches to this wild biker by completing all the details. Add heavy shading to his helmet, gloves, and boots. When you're done, outline the rest of Hulkoid's body with a felt-tip pen.

4. Erase unnecessary guidelines as you blend the shapes together. Carefully curve all the body lines as you define the muscles. Then start adding details to Hulkoid's face, body, and bike.

BAD-MAGIC MARVIN

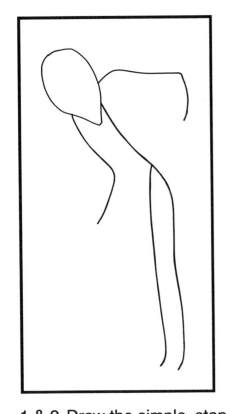

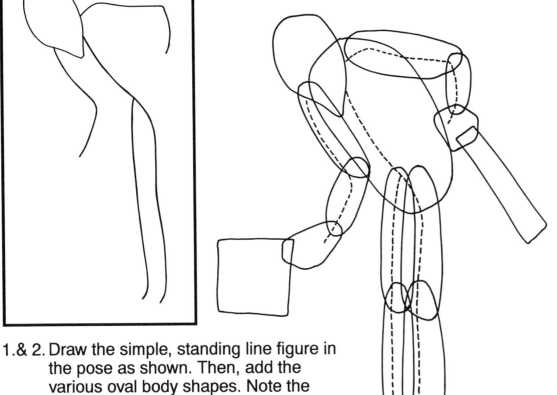

1.& 2. Draw the simple, standing line figure in the pose as shown. Then, add the various oval body shapes. Note the rectangular guidelines for Marvin's hat and cane.

3. Sketch the body parts within the oval guidelines, erasing the stick figure as you go along. Begin forming the hands and facial features, and create guidelines for his jacket, ruffles, and flowing hair.

Make sure you have built a solid foundation with the first two steps before continuing.

5. Finish Mad Marvin's clothes and face, and add all the final details so this supervillain can make his ghostly friend disappear.

4. Blend the body shapes together and complete the face, vest, jacket, hat, and cane.

If you're not satisfied with the way any part of your drawing looks, erase it and start again.

VILLAINELLA

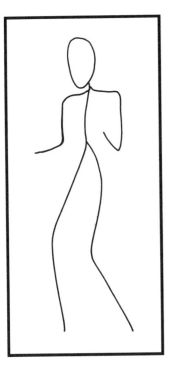

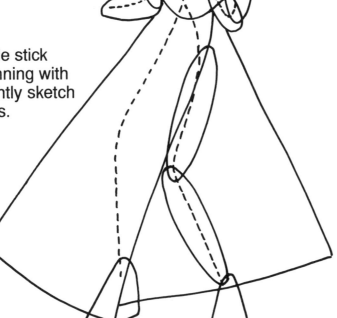

1.& 2. Start with the simple stick figure. Then, beginning with the upper body, lightly sketch all the basic shapes.

3. Draw guidelines for her hands, hair, facial features and cape. Begin forming her skirt and leg, as shown. Remember to erase any unnecessary line as you continue to refine your drawing.

4. Blend the guidelines together, and finish the face and hair. Note the curved mouth. Complete the fingers, clothes, and cape, and start adding details.

5. Continue adding details to the clothes as you continue to refine your drawing. Keep erasing and sketching until you're satisfied with the way Villainella looks. Use a thick marker to give her hair a dramatic look.

THE EVIL ROBO BAT

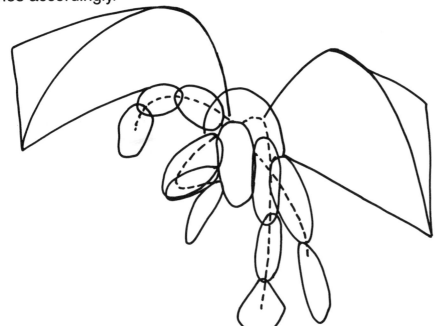

1. & 2. Lightly draw the stick figure and all the guideline shapes around it. This super-villain has huge wings, so draw your lines accordingly.

3. First, lightly sketch the body parts within the oval shapes, paying careful attention to the hands, feet, and wings. Next, start creating the head, erasing any lines you no longer need.

4. Complete the head and wings. Some of the parts of Robo Bat's body **don't** blend together, they butt into each other. Note how the tips of his wings curl to match his fangs and fingers.

5. For the finishing touches, add lots of lines all over the bat's body, face, and wings, giving him a real "robo" appearance.

These are just a few of the weapons
that you can add to any of your super-villainous drawings.
Use your imagination and create many more.

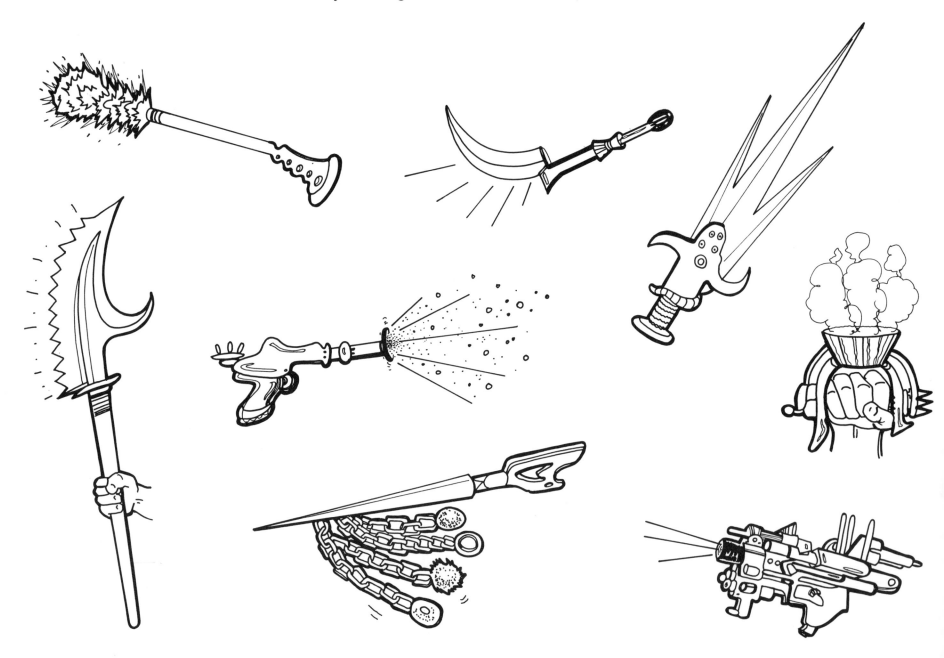

Algebra II Practice

BY

DR. BARBARA SANDALL, Ed.D.
DR. MELFRIED OLSON, Ed.D.
TRAVIS OLSON, M.S.

COPYRIGHT © 2006 Mark Twain Media, Inc.

ISBN 10-digit: 1-58037-326-7
        13-digit: 978-1-58037-326-5

Printing No. CD-404043

Mark Twain Media, Inc., Publishers
Distributed by Carson-Dellosa Publishing LLC

Visit us at www.carsondellosa.com

This product has been correlated to state, national, and Canadian provincial standards. Visit www.carsondellosa.com to search and view its correlations to your standards.

Table of Contents

Introduction to the Math Practice Books Series

The *Math Practice Books Series* will introduce students in middle school and high school to the course topics of Pre-algebra, Algebra, Algebra II, and Geometry. All of the practice books are aligned with the National Council of Teachers of Mathematics (NCTM) *Principles and Standards for School Mathematics.* (NCTM 2000)

This series is written for classroom teachers, parents, families, and students. The practice books in this series can be used as a full unit of study or as individual lessons to supplement textbooks or curriculum programs. Parents and students can use this series as an enhancement to what is being done in the classroom or as a tutorial at home. Students will be given a basic overview of the concepts, examples, practice problems, and challenge problems using the concepts introduced in the section. At the end of each section, there will be a set of problems to check progress on the concepts and a challenge set of problems over the whole section. At the end of the book, there will be problems for each section, which could be used for assessment.

According to the Mathematics Education Trust and NCTM, new technologies require that the fundamentals of algebra and algebraic thinking should be a part of the background for all citizens. These technologies also provide opportunities to generate numerical examples, graph data, analyze patterns, and make generalizations. An understanding of algebra is also important because business and industry require higher levels of thinking and problem solving. NCTM also suggests that understanding geometry, including the characteristics and properties of two and three-dimensional shapes, spatial relationships, symmetry, and the use of visualization and spatial reasoning, can also be used in solving problems.

The NCTM *Standards* suggest that content and vocabulary are necessary but of equal importance are the processes of mathematics. The process skills described in the Standards include: problem solving, reasoning, communication, and connections. The practice books in this series will address both the content and processes of algebra and algebraic thinking and geometry. This worktext, *Algebra II Practice*, will help students transition from Algebra to Algebra II.

Common Mathematics Symbols and Terms

Term	Symbol/Definition	Example
Addition sign	+	$2 + 2 = 4$
Subtraction sign	−	$4 − 2 = 2$
Multiplication sign	x or a dot • or 2 numbers or letters together or parentheses	3×2 $2 • 2$ $2x$ $2(2)$
Division sign	÷ or a slash mark (/) or a horizontal fraction bar	$6 ÷ 2$ $4/2$ $\frac{4}{2}$
Equals or is equal to	=	$2 + 2 = 4$
Does Not Equal	≠	$5 ≠ 1$
Parentheses – symbol for grouping numbers	( )	$(2 \times 5) + 3 =$
Pi – a number that is approximately 22/7 or ≈ 3.14	π	$3.1415926…$
Negative number – to the left of zero on a number line	-	-3
Positive number – to the right of zero on a number line	+	$+4$
Less than	<	$2 < 4$
Greater than	>	$4 > 2$
Greater than or equal to	≥	$2 + 3 ≥ 4; 2 • 5 ≥ 10$
Less than or equal to	≤	$2 + 1 ≤ 4; 3 + 2 ≤ 5$
Is approximately	≈	$π ≈ 3.14$
Radical sign	$\sqrt[n]{}$ $\sqrt{}$ n represents the index, which is assumed to be 2, the square root, when there is none shown.	$\sqrt{9}$ The square root of 9 $\sqrt[3]{27}$ The cube root of 27
The nth power of a	a^n	$3^2 = 9$

Common Mathematics Symbols and Terms (cont.)

Variables	Are letters used for unknown numbers	$x + 8 = 12$ x is the variable representing the unknown number
Mathematical Sentence	Contains two mathematical phrases joined by an equals (=) or an inequality $\{\neq, <, >, \leq, \geq\}$ sign	$2 + 3 = 5$ $9 - 3 > 5$ $3x + 8 = 20$ $4 + 2 \neq 5$
Equation	Mathematical sentence in which two phrases are connected with an equals (=) sign.	$5 + 7 = 12$ $3x = 12$ $1 = 1$
Mathematical Operations	Mathematics has four basic operations: addition, subtraction, multiplication, and division. Symbols are used for each operation.	+ sign indicates addition − sign indicates subtraction ÷ indicates division • or x indicates multiplication
Like Terms	Terms that contain the same variables with the same exponents and differ only in their coefficients	$3, 4, 5$ $3c, -5c, \frac{1}{2}c$ the variable is the same with the same exponent; they are like terms.
Unlike Terms	Terms with different variables, or terms with the same variable but different exponents	$5 + a$ Cannot be added because they are unlike terms $3x + 4y + 1z$ Cannot be added because the variables are different, so they are unlike terms
Coefficient	The number in front of the variable, that is, the numerical part of a term	$5x$ In this number, 5 is the coefficient
Identity Property of Addition	Any number or variable added to zero remains unchanged.	$0 + 5 = 5$ $-3 + 0 = -3$ $a + (4 - 4) = (a + 4) - 4 = a$
Identity Property of Multiplication	Any number or variable multiplied by one remains unchanged.	$12 \cdot 1 = 12$ $b \cdot 1 = b$ $3y \cdot \left(\frac{2}{2}\right) = \frac{6y}{2} = \left(\frac{1}{2}\right) \cdot 6y = 3y$

Common Mathematics Symbols and Terms (cont.)

Commutative Property of Addition	No matter the order in which you add two numbers, the sum is always the same.	$4 + 7 = 7 + 4$ $b + c = c + b$
Commutative Property of Multiplication	No matter the order in which you multiply two numbers, the answer is always the same.	$20 \times \frac{1}{2} = \frac{1}{2} \times 20$ $5 \bullet 3 = 3 \bullet 5$ $a \bullet b = b \bullet a$
Associative Property of Addition	When you add three numbers together, the sum will be the same no matter how you group the numbers.	$(5 + 6) + 7 = 5 + (6 + 7)$ $(a + b) + c = a + (b + c)$
Associative Property of Multiplication	No matter how you group the numbers when you multiply, the answer will always be the same product.	$(5 \bullet 4) \bullet 8 = 5 \bullet (4 \bullet 8)$ $(a \bullet b) \bullet c = a \bullet (b \bullet c)$
Distributive Property of Multiplication Over Addition	Allows the choice of multiplication followed by addition or addition followed by multiplication.	$3(5 + 2) = 3 \bullet 5 + 3 \bullet 2$ $a(b + c) = a \bullet b + a \bullet c$
Inverse Operation	Operation that undoes another operation	Multiplication and division $5 \bullet x = 5x$ $\dfrac{5x}{5} = x$ Addition and Subtraction $n + 5 - 5 = n$
Reciprocal or Multiplicative Inverse Property	Two reciprocals are multiplied, and the product is 1.	For any non-zero number: $\text{Number} \times \dfrac{1}{\text{Number}} = 1$ $\dfrac{1}{\text{Number}} \times \text{Number} = 1$ $a \bullet \dfrac{1}{a} = 1$ $5 \bullet \dfrac{1}{5} = 1$

Common Mathematics Symbols and Terms (cont.)

Exponents	Shorthand for repeated multiplication	$a^2 = a \cdot a$ $y^4 = y \cdot y \cdot y \cdot y$
Square Numbers	The result of multiplying a number or variable by itself	$4 \cdot 4 = 16$ $a \cdot a = a^2$
Square Roots	A square root indicated by the radical sign $\sqrt{}$ is the positive number multiplied by itself to get the radicand.	$\sqrt{9}$ What positive number multiplied by itself = 9? $3 \cdot 3 = 9$ So $\sqrt{9} = 3$
Radicand	Number under the radical	$\sqrt{9}$ 9 is the radicand
Index	Number inside the crook of the radical sign that tells which root of the radicand is being calculated. When it is not written, the index is assumed to be 2.	$\sqrt[3]{125}$ The index 3 tells us that the cube root or the third root is being sought. Since $5^3 = 125$, then $\sqrt[3]{125} = 5$.
Numerator	Top number of a fraction	$\frac{3}{5}$ In this fraction, 3 is the numerator.
Denominator	Bottom number of a fraction	$\frac{3}{5}$ In this fraction, 5 is the denominator.
Integers	Zero, the natural numbers, and their opposites—the negative integers	Set of integers: $\{...-3,-2,-1,0,1,2,3...\}$
Additive Inverse Property of Addition	The sum of an integer and its opposite integer will always be zero.	$a + (-a) = 0$ $-5 + 5 = 0$
Set	A well-defined collection of numbers, elements, or objects	Set of integers: $\{...-3,-2,-1,0,1,2,3...\}$

Common Mathematics Symbols and Terms (cont.)

Absolute Value	The absolute value of a number can be considered as the distance between the number and zero on the number line. The absolute value of every number will be either positive or zero. Real numbers come in paired opposites, *a* and -*a*, that are the same distance from the origin but in opposite directions. ![number line -3 to 3]	Absolute value of *a*: $\|a\| = a$ if *a* is positive $\|a\| = a$ if *a* is negative $\|a\| = 0$ if *a* is 0 With 0 as the **origin** on the number line, the absolute value of both -3 and +3 is equal to 3, because both numbers are 3 units in distance from the origin.
Expression	Any collection of numbers, variables, or terms with grouping symbols and mathematical operators.	$-3xy$ $2ab + b$ $2z + 4c + 2 - y$ $5[(x+3)^2 - 4b] + 2h$
Monomial	A polynomial with one term	$-x^3$ $14x$ -0.2
Binomial	A polynomial with two terms	$2x^2 - 5x$ $x^3 + 2.4x$ $x + 3$ $2 - 7x$
Polynomial in One Variable	Is an expression containing the sum of a finite number of terms of the form ax^n, for any real number *a* and any whole number *n*	$-2x^2 + 6x + 3$ $x - \frac{3}{8}$ $x^3 + 2.4x - 1$ $3x^5 - x^4 + 5x^2 + 3x - 9$

Common Mathematics Symbols and Terms (cont.)

Function	A special type of relation in which no two ordered pairs have the same first coordinate and have a different second coordinate. A function can be thought of as a rule that takes an input value from the domain and returns an output value in the range. A function can be indicated by a set of ordered pairs or by a graph in the plane.	Example 1: $y = 0.5x + 2$ Example 2: We choose a value of x and calculate the corresponding value for y. The function consists of the set of ordered pairs: $\{(x, 0.5x + 2)\}$. <table><tr><td>x</td><td>y</td></tr><tr><td>-1</td><td>0</td></tr><tr><td>5</td><td>6</td></tr><tr><td>0</td><td>1</td></tr><tr><td>7</td><td>8</td></tr></table>
Ordered Pair	Describes a point in the coordinate plane. The first number of the pair tells the location relative to the x-axis, and the second tells the location of the point relative to the y-axis.	(3, 8) - three to the right of 0 on the x-axis (x-coordinate); 8 up on the y-axis (y-coordinate). The point is where these two intersect.
Relation	Defined as any set of ordered pairs $\{(x, y)\}$. A relation can be indicated by an equation in two variables or by a graph in the plane.	$x + y^2 = y + 2$ $xy = 1$ $\{(-2, 3), (0, 4), (3, 3), (0, -1)\}$ $y = -2x^2 + 6x + 3$
Domain	Set from which an input value can be chosen for the independent variable, that is, the first coordinate of an ordered pair in a relation	$\{(5, -6), (10, 7), (-2, 0)\}$ The set $\{5, 10, -2\}$ is the domain for this relation.
Range	Set of all second-coordinate values of the dependent variable used in the ordered pair in a relation	$\{(5, -6), (10, 7), (-2, 0)\}$ The set $\{-6, 7, 0\}$ is the range for this relation.
Function Notation	$f(x)$ is read as "f of x" or "f at x" and means "f evaluated at the value x."	If $f(x) = 2x^2 - 5x$, then "$f(4)$ means to substitute 4 into the function for x, that is, $f(4) = 2 \bullet (4)^2 - 5 \bullet (4) = 12$
Comparison Property	For any two real numbers, a and b, exactly one of these statements is true. $a < b$ $a = b$ $a > b$	$9 < 11$ $7 = 7$ $-3 > -5$

Common Mathematics Symbols and Terms (cont.)

Transitive Property	If $a < b$ and $b < c$, then $a < c$.	$3 < 10 < 12$
Addition Property	If $a < b$, then $a + c < b + c$	$4 < 6$ $4 + 2 < 6 + 2$
Multiplication Property	If $a < b$ and c is a positive number, then $ac < bc$. If $a < b$ and c is a negative number, then $ac > bc$.	$4 < 6$ $4(2) < 6(2)$ $4 < 6$ $4(-2) > 6(-2)$
Conjunction	A sentence formed by joining two sentences with the word *and*. A conjunction is true only when both sentences are true.	$x > -2$ and $x < 3$
Disjunction	A sentence formed by joining two sentences with the word *or*. A disjunction is true if at least one of the sentences is true.	$x < 2$ or $x = 2$
Open Sentences	An equation or inequality that contains one or more variables.	$x < 9$ $x = 4 + y$
Solution Set	Set of all solutions for an open sentence	$x < 9$ Solution set: $\{8, 7, 6, ...\}$
Constant	A number with a precise value	$-3, \frac{1}{2}, 0, \pi, \sqrt{5}$
Degree of a Variable	Number of times the variable is a factor	$3x^3$ Degree of x is 3 $2y^2$ Degree of y is 2
Degree of a Monomial	Sum of the exponents of all the variables in the monomial	$3ab^3$ is degree 4, since a is degree 1 and b^3 is degree 3
Similar Monomials Also called **Like Monomials**	Monomials with the same variables and the same exponents that may differ in their coefficients	ab^3 and $3ab^3$ are similar ab^2 and $3ab^3$ are not similar
Simplified Polynomial	Polynomial that has no two terms that are similar. The terms are usually arranged in order of decreasing degree of one of the variables.	$3x^3 + 2x^2 + 4x - 1$

Common Mathematics Symbols and Terms (cont.)

Degree of Polynomial	The greatest of the degrees of its terms after it has been simplified. The process of writing a polynomial as a product of prime coefficients, and prime monomials, and prime binomials, etc.	$3x^3 + 2x^2y^2 + 4x - 1$ $3x^3$ (degree is 3) + $2x^2y^2$ (degree is 4 because you add the 2 exponents) + $4x$ (degree is 1) $- 1$ (0 has no degree). The highest degree then is 4, so the degree of this polynomial is 4. $10x^2 - 90y^2$ $= 2 \bullet 5 \bullet (x - 3y \bullet (x + 3y)$
Prime Factorization	The process of writing a positive integer as a product of primes The process of writing a polynomial as a product of prime coeficients, prime monomials, and prime binomials, etc.	$24 = 2 \bullet 2 \bullet 2 \bullet 3$ $10x^2 - 90y^2$ $= 2 \bullet 5 \bullet (x - 3y) \bullet (x + 3y)$
Greatest Common Factor (GCF)	The largest positive integer that will divide each number from a given set of numbers. A monomial that divides every term of a given polynomial or other set of monomials	2 is the GCF of {6, -8, 12} $3x^2$ is the GCF of $15x^5 - 12x^3 + 3x^2$
Least Common Multiple (LCM)	The smallest positive integer that can be divided by each number from a given set of numbers The monomial of least degree with the smallest coefficient that can be divided by each monomial from a given set The polynomial of least degree with the smallest coefficient that can be divided by each polynomial from a given set	72 is the LCM of {6, -8, 12} $12a^3$ is the LCM of $\{2a, 4a^3, 6a^2\}$ $30x^3(2 - y)^2$ is the LCM of $\{3x(2 - y), 10x^3, 5x^2(2 - y)^2\}$
Factor Set	Set from which numbers or polynomials are chosen as factors	The factor set for 14 is $\{(1)(14), (-1)(-14), (2)(7), (2-)(-7)\}$
Prime Number	An integer greater than 1 whose only positive factors are 1 and itself.	2, 3, 5, 7, etc.

Algebra Rules and Laws

Rule	Description	Examples
Integer Subtraction Rule	For all integers a and b: $a - b = a + (-b)$	$12 - 5 = 12 + (-5)$
Addition Property of Equality	The same number, positive or negative, can be added to both sides of an equation without changing the solution(s) of the equation.	$2y - 1 = 6$ $2y - 1 + 1 = 6 + 1$ $4x + 2 = 10$ $4x + 2 - 2 = 10 - 2$
Multiplication Property of Equality	Each term on both sides of an equation can be multiplied or divided by the same non-zero number without changing the solution(s) of the equation.	$\frac{x}{6} = 3 \implies 6 \cdot \left(\frac{x}{6}\right) = 6 \cdot 3$ $4n = 8 \implies \frac{4n}{4} = \frac{8}{4}$
Laws of Exponents	Let a and b be real numbers and n and m be positive integers: $a^m \cdot a^n = a^{m+n}$ $(ab)^m = a^m b^m$ $(a^m)^n = a^{mn}$ If $m > n$, $\dfrac{a^m}{a^n} = a^{m-n}$ If $n > m$, $\dfrac{a^m}{a^n} = \dfrac{1}{a^{n-m}}$	$x^2 \cdot x^3 = x^{2+3} = x^5$ $(xy)^2 = x^2 y^2$ $(c^2)^3 = c^{2(3)} = c^6$ $\dfrac{x^5}{x^3} = x^{5-3} = x^2$ $\dfrac{y^2}{y^5} = \dfrac{1}{y^{5-2}} = \dfrac{1}{y^3}$

Name: _____ Date: _____

Chapter 1: Solving Equations and Problems

Basic Overview: Simplifying Expressions and Solving Equations With One Variable

Algebraic expressions can be simplified by applying the Order of Operations, particularly when the expressions contain multiple operations. (1) First evaluate within parentheses from innermost to outermost using rules 2, 3, and 4 in order; (2) Evaluate all exponents; (3) Multiply and/or divide from left to right; and then (4) Add and/or subtract, also from left to right.

Equations can sometimes be solved by the guess-and-check method, but more often their solutions follow directly from using the principles of algebra. Equations can be systematically solved, as follows: (1) Use the distributive property to remove parentheses and simplify each side of the equation; (2) Apply the addition property of equality to variables on one side of the equation and constants on the other side; and (3) Apply the multiplication property of equality to isolate the variable.

Examples of Simplifying Expressions and Solving Equations With One Variable

Example of Simplifying Algebraic Expressions:

$$3 \bullet (4 + 5) = 3 \bullet (9) = 27 \qquad \text{Order of Operations}$$

Example of Simplifying Equations With One Variable by Addition and Subtraction:

$$x - 4 = 9$$
$$(x - 4) + 4 = 9 + 4 \qquad \text{Addition Property of Equality}$$
$$x + (-4 + 4) = 13 \qquad \text{Associative Property of Addition}$$
$$x = 13 \qquad \text{Identity Property of Addition}$$

Example of Simplifying Equations With One Variable by Multiplication and Division:

$$7b = 5(6 + 1)$$

$$\frac{7b}{7} = \frac{35}{7}$$

$$b = 5$$

Name: _____ Date: _____

Chapter 1: Solving Equations and Problems (cont.)

Practice: Simplifying Expressions and Solving Equations With One Variable

Directions: Simplify the following expressions.

1. $7x - 2 + 3(x - 9) + 5$ _____

2. $40 \div 4 - 3(9 - 2)$ _____

3. $2^2 - 5(x + 3)$ _____

4. $2(x - 5) + 3(x + 11) - x$ _____

5. $3x - 6(2 - x) + 3(x - 2) + 8$ _____

6. $a - 2a - [3a - (4a - 5)]$ _____

7. $3^3a - 2^4a + 7a - 2(9 - a)$ _____

8. $13(5 - t) - (5 - t) - 12(5 - t)$ _____

Directions: Simplify and solve the following equations. Work the problem on your own paper, if you need more room.

9. $2a + 3a - 13 = a + 3$

10. $3(x - 55) = 0$

11. $3(x - 55) + 22 = x + 55$

12. $5 - 2x + 9 - 3 = 3x + 2$

13. If $8x + 5(3 + x) - a = 15 + 5x$, then $a = ?$ _____

14. $3x + 4(x - 3) = 6x - 9$

15. $5t - (4 - t) = 8 - (2 + t)$

Name: _____ Date: _____

Chapter 1: Solving Equations and Problems (cont.)

16. $17(2x + 3) = 15(2x + 3)$

    _____

17. $3x + 4x = 6(2x - 1)$

    _____

18. $18 - 4^2(1 - 3x) = 98$

    _____

19. $3 - 5(x + 9) = 3$

    _____

20. $12 + [5 - (9 + 2x)] = 7 - 5x$

    _____

Challenge Problems: Simplifying Expressions and Solving Equations With One Variable

Directions: Work the problems on your own paper, and write the answers on the lines below.

1. Simplify. $2x - \{2 - [2(x - 2) - (2 - x)]\}$

   _____

2. If $3x + 5(x - 2) + a = 9x + 13$, then $a = ?$

   _____

3. Simplify. $3[5^2 - 5(14 \div 7) + 9^0 - 8]$

   _____

4. Simplify and solve. $22x + 9(2 - 3x) = 3(2 - 3x)$

   _____

5. Simplify and solve. $43(19 - 7x) + 32(19 - 7x) = 25(7x - 19)$

   _____

Chapter 1: Solving Equations and Problems (cont.)

Basic Overview: Changing Words Into Symbols; Problem Solving With Equations

Word problems describe relationships between or among number ideas and specific arithmetic operations. We often transform verbal problems into algebraic expressions quite naturally. To support this process, practice the following steps:

(1) **Read the problem carefully** to identify the quantities you are being asked to find;

(2) If possible, **draw a sketch** to help visualize the problem;

(3) **Choose a variable** and use it to express the unknown quantities;

(4) **Write the equation** that represents the problem statement;

(5) **Solve the equation** and answer the questions being asked; and

(6) **Check your solution** in your original equation.

Examples of Changing Words Into Symbols; Problem Solving With Equations

Example of Changing Word Phrases Into Algebraic Expressions:

A number is increased by 5
"A number" is replaced with the letter a
$a + 5$

Example of Changing Sentences Into Algebraic Expressions:

If a runner runs at x miles/hour, what would his speed be
if he was 2 miles per hour slower?
Speed = x
"2 miles an hour slower" is represented by -2
$x + (-2) = x - 2$

Example of Changing Scientific Formulas Into Algebraic Equations:

The amount of work done is represented by the formula:
    Work = force times distance or $W = f \bullet d$.

How much work was done if a force of 25 kg was moved a distance of 6 m?

W = work done   Force f = 25 kg   Distance d = 6 m
W = 25 kg $\bullet$ 6 m

Chapter 1: Solving Equations and Problems (cont.)

Example of Using a Variable as an Unknown and Writing an Equation to Represent the Situation:

Your class has 24 students. The number of boys is 4 less than twice the number of girls. How would you write an algebraic equation to represent these statements?

(Number of girls = g) + (Number of boys is represented by $2g - 4$) = 24

$g + (2g - 4) = 24$ $\Rightarrow$ $3g - 4 = 24$

Example of Problem Solving With Equations:

Tickets to a major league game were $100 for a box seat and $50 for a bleacher seat. There were 1,000 more bleacher seats sold than box seats. If the total of ticket sales was $62,000, how many of each ticket were sold?

Let b represent the number of box seats.

Money from the box tickets sold + money from the bleacher tickets sold = total sales

$\$100 \cdot b + \$50(b + 1{,}000) = \$62{,}000$

$100b + 50b + 50{,}000 = 62{,}000$
$150b + 50{,}000 = 62{,}000$
$150b + 50{,}000 - 50{,}000 = 62{,}000 - 50{,}000$
$150b = 12{,}000$
$\dfrac{150b}{150} = \dfrac{12{,}000}{150}$
$b = 80$ box seats were sold

The number of bleacher seats is 1,000 more than the box seats.
Bleacher seats = $b + 1{,}000$

The number of bleacher seats is 80 + 1,000 = 1,080.

Name: _____ Date: _____

Chapter 1: Solving Equations and Problems (cont.)

Practice: Changing Words Into Symbols; Problem Solving With Equations

Directions: Write an equation for the problem and then solve.

1. Nine less than five times a number is 86. What is the number?

   _____

2. Twenty-two pencils cost $0.60 less than $5. What is the cost per pencil?

   _____

3. Nathan bought 12 pairs of bookends. If he paid a total of $204 for all the bookends, how much was the cost of each pair of bookends?

   _____

4. Hamilton High School has 90 students in the 11th grade. There are 6 more girls than boys. How many boys and how many girls are there?

   _____

5. Irene received $425 in annual interest on a principal investment sum of $5,000. What was the simple interest rate for this return?

   _____

6. The area of the Red Sea, 453,000 km², is approximately 18% of the area of the Mediterranean Sea. What is the approximate area of the Mediterranean Sea?

   _____

7. Linda's Aunt Zoe charges her a nominal amount for watching her two children. Aunt Zoe charges $2.50 per day plus $1.75 per hour. One day Linda paid her aunt $14.75. How many hours did Aunt Zoe watch the children?

   _____

Name: _____   Date: _____

Chapter 1: Solving Equations and Problems (cont.)

8. Varisoon has various rates for long distance phone service. On her plan, Noslo is charged 0.045 per minute and $4.95 per month. During the month of December, Noslo's bill was $22.95 for the long distance service. How many minutes did Noslo use?

_____

9. Noslo also has cell phone service from Varisoon Wireless. She pays a flat fee of $39.95 for 350 minutes per month. Any minutes over 350 are at an additional cost. In November, Noslo's bill for wireless service was $108.70 for 475 minutes. What is the charge per minute for the minutes over 350 per month?

_____

10. Kevala sells sodas and sundaes at his food stand. One week the number of sodas he made was 4 fewer than 5 times the number of sundaes. If he made 96 sodas, how many sundaes did he make?

_____

11. The perimeters of two rectangles are equal. The dimensions of one rectangle are 2x and x while the dimensions of the other rectangle are $x + 12$ and $x - 3$. What are the numerical dimensions of the rectangles?

_____

12. The number of trees sold by Star Market in April was 3 more than twice the number of trees sold in March. If seventy-one trees were sold in April, how many trees were sold in March?

_____

13. Torrey has a coin collection from his foreign travels to Sweden and Norway. He has a total of 998 coins. The number of Norwegian coins is 26 fewer than three times the number of Swedish coins. How many coins from each country does he have?

_____

14. Larry, Moe, and Curly were running for student council. Moe got twice as many votes as Larry. Curly won the election with 7 more votes than Moe. If 327 people voted, how many votes did each person get?

_____

Chapter 1: Solving Equations and Problems (cont.)

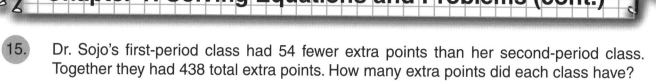

15. Dr. Sojo's first-period class had 54 fewer extra points than her second-period class. Together they had 438 total extra points. How many extra points did each class have?

_____

16. Wendy is a painter. She charged $310 for the paint plus $16 per hour to paint a house. Her bill was $790. How many hours did she work?

_____

17. Rudy runs a small business during the summer making hamster cages. He makes 8 cages per day. He charges $9 for each cage that he sells, but must pay his mom $1.35 per cage for materials. One month he earned $918. How many days did he work?

_____

18. Eric is fencing his mom's rectangular-shaped garden. The garden is 50 feet longer than it is wide, and he used 340 feet of fencing. What are the dimensions of the garden?

_____

19. Sue was to make a triangle with these conditions. One angle was to be double the other, with the third being 5 degrees more than one-half of the smaller of the other two. What were the angle measures in the triangle Sue made?

_____

20. The area of a triangle is 48 square meters. If the length of the base is 24 meters, what is the height of the triangle?

_____

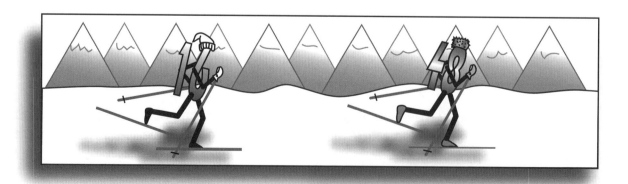

Name: _____   Date: _____

Chapter 1: Solving Equations and Problems (cont.)

Challenge Problems: Changing Words Into Symbols, Problem Solving With Equations

Directions: Write an equation for the problem and then solve.

1. Change this phrase into symbols. Nine more than "twice the value of a number decreased by 6".

    _____

2. If the pep squad at Math High School (MHS) must pay the manufacturer $75 for the design of a pennant and $3 per pennant made, write an expression that represents the total that MHS must pay to have q pennants made.

    _____

3. Two angles are supplementary. The larger is 60° less than twice the smaller. What are the measures of the angles?

    _____

4. Find three consecutive numbers such that twice the sum of the first two is 9 more than three times the third.

    _____

5. The denominator of a certain fraction exceeds its numerator by 5. If the denominator is decreased by 3 and the numerator is increased by 1, the resulting fraction has the value of $\frac{4}{5}$. What is the fraction?

    _____

Name: _____ Date: _____

Chapter 1: Solving Equations and Problems (cont.)

Checking Progress: Solving Equations and Problems

1. Simplify. $-3x - 6(2 - 3x) - 3(x - 2) - 9$ _____

2. Simplify. $1.3(5 + 7t) - 0.1(5 + 7t) - 1.2(5 + 7t)$ _____

3. If $7x + [-5(3 - x)] - a = 12 + 3x$, then $a = ?$ _____

4. Solve. $-4^2 - (-9 - 7x) = 98$ _____

5. Solve. $2 - [5 - (9 + 5x)] = -(7 - 6x)$ _____

6. Solve. $422(1 - 19x) + 3.92(1 - 19x) = \frac{3}{8}(19x - 1)$

   _____

7. Hamilton High School has 190 students in the 11th and 12th grades. There are 16 more students in grade 11 than in grade 12. How many students are there in each grade?

   _____

8. Noslo has cell phone service from Varisoon Wireless. She pays a flat fee of $39.95 for 350 minutes per month. Any minutes over 350 are at an additional cost. In November, Noslo's bill for wireless service was $72.95 for 500 minutes. What is the charge per minute for the minutes over 350 per month?

   _____

9. Wendy is a painter. She charged $340 for the paint plus $14 per hour to paint a house. Her bill was $732. How many hours did she work?

   _____

10. Sue constructed a triangle as follows: the second angle was 2° less than twice the measure of the first angle, and the third was 7° more than one-half the measure of the first angle. What are the angle measures of the triangle that Sue created?

    _____

Name: _____ Date: _____

Chapter 2: Inequalities

Basic Overview: Inequalities

Symbols for inequalities include:

Greater than	>
Less than	<
Greater than or equal to	≥
Less than or equal to	≤

A **simple inequality** is a statement that two algebraic expressions are not equal in a particular way. Inequalities are written using any of the four symbols above. The first two are called **strict inequalities** (> and <), and the latter two are referred to as **inclusive inequalities** (≥ and ≤).

Replacing the equal sign in the general linear equation $ax + b = 0$ by any of the four symbols results in a linear inequality. The solution set to a simple inequality is the set of all real numbers for which the inequality is true. To solve linear inequalities, we use techniques similar to those used in solving linear equations. The Addition Property of Equality is applied exactly the same to inequalities as it is to equations. The Multiplication Property of Equality is also applied exactly the same when the inequality is multiplied or divided on both sides by a positive number. However, when an inequality is multiplied or divided on both sides by a negative number, the direction of the inequality is reversed.

To graph the solution set for a **linear inequality**: (1) Locate the number on the number line; (2) If the symbol is **strict**, place a circle (○) on the number's location, and if the symbol is **inclusive**, place a dot (●) on the number's location; and (3) Shade the right or left half-line that represents the solution set.

A **compound inequality** is a sentence containing two simple inequalities connected with *and* or *or*. A **conjunction** is a sentence formed by joining two simple inequalities with the word *and*. A conjunction is true only when both sides of the sentence are true. A **disjunction** is a sentence formed by joining two simple inequalities with the word *or*. A disjunction is true if at least one side of the sentence is true.

A simple inequality that includes an absolute value expression can be solved by first changing it to either a conjunction or disjunction sentence.

Examples of Inequalities

Examples of True Inequalities:

$4 > 2$	$-3 ≥ -6$	$2 < 10$	$5 ≤ 5$

Name: _____ Date: _____

Chapter 2: Inequalities (cont.)

Challenge Problems: Inequalities

1. T or F? $3 - a < 5 - a$

2. T or F? $a > a$

3. T or F? $0 < a$ for all values of a

4. What is the smallest integer value of x such that $3x \geq -12$?

    _____

5. Solve the inequality. $3x - 2 < 5$ or $2x + 3 < 7$

    _____

6. Solve the inequality. $3x - 2 < 5$ and $2x + 3 < 7$

    _____

7. Solve the inequality. $41(x - 3) < 99(x - 3)$

    _____

8. Solve the inequality. $-x > 3$ and $x > 5$

    _____

9. Solve the inequality. $2 + 3x > 3x + 2$

    _____

10. Solve the absolute value. $\left| \frac{3}{5}x + 9 \right| \geq 21$

    _____

Name: _____ Date: _____

Chapter 2: Inequalities (cont.)

Checking Progress: Inequalities

1. T or F? $2 + 5(2) > 7 + 9$

2. T or F? If $x > 0$, $9x + 443 > 12x + 443$

3. Graph on a number line. $-b \leq 9$

4. Graph on a number line. $2x < 3 - 4 - 5$

5. Solve. $-2x + 14 < 8 - 3x$

   _____

6. $18(x + 5) < 9(x + 5)$

   _____

7. $x < 19$ and $x < 23$

   _____

8. $2x + 3 > 6$ or $3 - 2x < 7$

   _____

9. $|x + 8| \geq 2$

   _____

10. $|0.5x - 3| \leq 5$

   _____

Name: _____ Date: _____

Chapter 3: Linear Equations and Inequalities

Basic Overview: Linear Equations and Graphs

A **linear equation in one variable** is any equation that can be put into the general form, $ax + b = 0$, where a and b are real numbers with $a \neq 0$. The solution to a linear equation is the number that makes the equation a true statement. There are two properties of linear equations that guide our use of the four arithmetic operations when attempting to solve a linear equation.

Addition Property of Equality

The same number can be added to both sides of an equation without changing the solution. Subtraction is defined in terms of addition $[a - b = a + (-b)]$, hence, the same number can be subtracted from both sides of an equation without changing the solution.

Multiplication Property of Equality

Both sides of an equation can be multiplied by the same non-zero number without changing the solution. Since division can be defined in terms of multiplication $\left(\frac{a}{b}\right.$ means $\left. a \cdot \frac{1}{b}\right)$, both sides of an equation can be divided by the same non-zero number without changing the solution.

When solving linear equations, follow these steps:
- Use the distributive property to remove parentheses as you utilize the order of operations.
- Use the addition property to rewrite the equation with all terms containing the variable on one side, and all terms without a variable on the other side. After combining like terms, you should get an equation of the form, $ax = b$.
- Use the multiplication property to isolate the variable. This step will give a solution of the form, $x =$ some number.
- Check your solution in the original equation.

A **linear equation in two variables** is an equation that can be put into the form $ax + by = c$, where a, b, and c are real numbers, and a and b are not both zero. The solution set for this type of linear equation is the set of all ordered pairs $\{(x, y)\}$ of real numbers that make the equation true. The graph of a linear equation is always a straight line in the coordinate grid, and it is a representation of all of the points, that is, ordered pairs in the solution set.

Examples of Linear Equations and Graphs

Example of Using Linear Equations to Solve Problems:

$$3x + 9 = 108$$
$$3x + 9 - 9 = 108 - 9$$
$$3x = 99$$
$$\frac{3x}{3} = \frac{99}{3}$$
$$x = 33$$

Name: _____   Date: _____

Chapter 3: Linear Equations and Inequalities (cont.)

Example of Finding the Solution Set for a Linear Equation:

$$9x - 2y = 15 \quad \text{if } x \in \{-1, 0, 1, 2, 3\}$$
$$9x + 2y = 15$$
$$9x - 9x + 2y = 15 - 9x$$
$$2y = 15 - 9x$$
$$\frac{2y}{2} = \frac{15 - 9x}{2}$$
$$y = \frac{15 - 9x}{2}$$

SCOREBOARD

HOME		VISITORS	
y=0	y=1	y=2	y=3
15	15	15	15
-0	+9	-18	-27

If $x = -1$
$$y = \frac{15 - 9(-1)}{2}$$
$$y = \frac{15 + 9}{2}$$
$$y = \frac{24}{2}$$
$$y = 12$$

x	y	Solution Set
-1	12	(-1, 12)
0	$\frac{15}{2}$	$(0, \frac{15}{2})$
1	3	(1, 3)
2	$-\frac{3}{2}$	$(2, -\frac{3}{2})$
3	-6	(3, -6)

If $x = 0$
$$y = \frac{15 - 9(0)}{2}$$
$$y = \frac{15 - 0}{2}$$
$$y = \frac{15}{2}$$

If $x = 1$
$$y = \frac{15 - 9(1)}{2}$$
$$y = \frac{15 - 9}{2}$$
$$y = \frac{6}{2}$$
$$y = 3$$

If $x = 2$
$$y = \frac{15 - 9(2)}{2}$$
$$y = \frac{15 - 18}{2}$$
$$y = \frac{-3}{2}$$

If $x = 3$
$$y = \frac{15 - 9(3)}{2}$$
$$y = \frac{15 - 27}{2}$$
$$y = \frac{-12}{2}$$
$$y = -6$$

Then the solution set is $\left\{(-1, 12), \left(0, \frac{15}{2}\right), (1, 3), \left(2, -\frac{3}{2}\right), (3, -6)\right\}$.

Name: _____ Date: _____

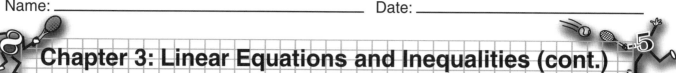

Chapter 3: Linear Equations and Inequalities (cont.)

Example of Linear Equations and Graphs:

$x - y = 0$ if $x \in \{-1, 0, 1, 5, -6\}$

x	y	Solution Set
-1	-1	(-1, -1)
0	0	(0, 0)
1	1	(1, 1)
5	5	(5, 5)
-6	-6	(-6, -6)

In the graph below, the points from the table above were plotted and connected to form the line that represents the solution set of the equation. Any point on the line represents an ordered pair, which is a solution to the equation.

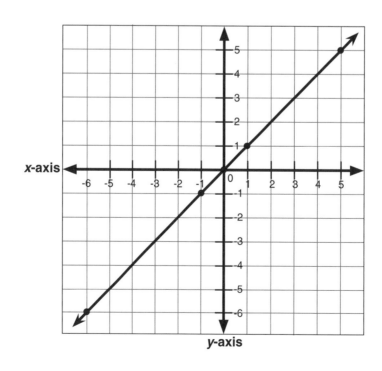

Name: _____   Date: _____

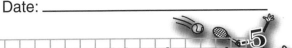

Chapter 3: Linear Equations and Inequalities (cont.)

Practice: Linear Equations and Graphs

Directions: Find the *y* values for the corresponding *x* values for each linear equation.

1. $y = 3 - 2x$

x	y
-2	
-1	
0	
1	
2	
5	
12	

2. $y = 3x + 4$

x	y
-2	
-1	
0	
1	
2	
5	
12	

3. $y = -3x + 4$

x	y
-2	
-1	
0	
1	
2	
5	
12	

4. $y = 0.5x - 5$

x	y
-2	
-1	
0	
1	
2	
5	
12	

5. $3x - 4y = 8$

x	y
-2	
-1	
0	
1	
2	
5	
12	

6. $2x + 5y = 15$

x	y
-2	
-1	
0	
1	
2	
5	
12	

Name: _____ Date: _____

Chapter 3: Linear Equations and Inequalities (cont.)

Directions: Find the *x* values for the corresponding *y* values for each linear equation.

7. $3x + 2y = 12$

x	y
	-5
	-2
	0
	1
	100

8. $5x - y = 10$

x	y
	-5
	-2
	0
	1
	100

9. $4x + 5y - 9 = 0$

x	y
	-5
	-2
	0
	1
	100

10. $3x - 0.5y = 13$

x	y
	-5
	-2
	0
	1
	100

11. $y = 5x - 4$

x	y
	-5
	-2
	0
	1
	100

12. $y = \frac{3}{5}x + 5$

x	y
	-5
	-2
	0
	1
	100

Directions: Graph the equations on your own graph paper.

13. $y = 0.5x - 5$

14. $y = 3 - 2x$

15. $y = -3x + 4$

16. $2x + 5y = 15$

17. $4x + 5y - 9 = 0$

18. $3x - 0.5y = 13$

19. $y = 5x - 4$

20. $y = \frac{3}{5}x + 5$

Name: _____ Date: _____

Chapter 3: Linear Equations and Inequalities (cont.)

Challenge Problems: Linear Equations and Graphs

Directions: Answer the following questions.

1. Evie said that for the equation $3x + 4y = 12$ the y-intercept was 3 because $12 \div 4 = 3$. Is she correct, and why?

   _____

   _____

2. Diane indicated that if she knew that $(0, 5)$ and $(2, 0)$ were points on a line, it was easy to write the slope-intercept form of the equation for the line. How could she be so certain?

   _____

   _____

3. When she was making a table of values for the equations $y = 3x + 5$ and $y = 3x + 9$, Rachel made an interesting discovery. What do you think it could have been?

   _____

   _____

4. When graphing equations, Tim was surprised to find that when he graphed $3x + 2y = 6$ and $6x + 4y = 12$, he got the same graph. Do you think he graphed the equations correctly?

   _____

   _____

5. Julian told Erin that the point $(48, 91)$ was a point on the line $2x + 3y = 369$ and challenged her to find another point. Within 10 seconds, using only mental arithmetic, Erin correctly gave Julian 5 points on the equation. How do you think Erin was able to do so that quickly?

   _____

   _____

Name: _____ Date: _____

Chapter 3: Linear Equations and Inequalities (cont.)

Basic Overview: Linear Inequalities

A **linear inequality in two variables** is simply a linear equation with the equal sign replaced by an inequality symbol. The graph of the solution set for an inequality is the half-plane of ordered pairs on one side of the line associated with the inequality. The line may or may not be included in the solution set, depending on the type of inequality being solved and graphed. If the sentence contains a strict inequality (> or <), draw a dotted line for the graph of the associated equation, which means the line is not included. If the sentence contains an inclusive inequality (≤ or ≥), draw a solid line graph, which indicates that the line is included in the solution set. Select any point not on the line and determine if that ordered pair satisfies the inequality. If yes, then all the points in that half-plane are in the solution set, and if no, then all the points in the other half-plane are in the solution set.

Example of Linear Inequalities and Graphs

Example of a Linear Inequality in Two Variables:

$y > \frac{1}{2}x + 1$

For this inequality, the associated equation is: $y = \frac{1}{2}x + 1$

The solution set includes the half-plane of ordered pairs above the line, but not any points on the line.

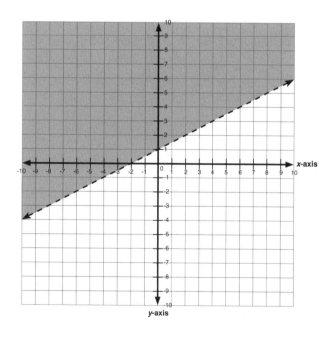

Name: _____ Date: _____

Chapter 3: Linear Equations and Inequalities (cont.)

Practice: Linear Inequalities and Graphs

Directions: Graph the following inequalities on your own graph paper.

1. $y < 5x + 2$

2. $3x + 2y > 6$

3. $4x + 5y - 20 > 0$

4. $4x - 5y - 20 > 0$

5. $-4x - 5y - 20 > 0$

6. $y \leq -2x + 5$

7. $y \geq 2x - 5$

8. $y + 5 \leq 2x$

9. $5y < 6x - 30$

10. $0 > 12 - 2x - 3y$

Challenge Problems: Linear Inequalities

Directions: Complete the following on your own graph paper.

1. On a coordinate grid, graph $y > 4$.

2. On a coordinate grid, what points satisfy both $y > 2$ and $x > 3$?

3. On a coordinate grid, what points satisfy both $3x + 2y > 6$ and $3x + 2y < 12$?

Name: _____ Date: _____

Chapter 3: Linear Equations and Inequalities (cont.)

Example of Solving Systems of Equations With Unrelated Coefficients:

$$2x - 5y = 2 \qquad -5x + 3y = 4$$

$$-5(2x - 5y = 2)$$
$$-5(2x) - 5(-5y) = -5(2)$$
$$-10x + 25y = -10$$

$$2(-5x + 3y = 4)$$
$$2(-5x) + 2(3y) = 2(4)$$
$$-10x + 6y = 8$$

$$-10x + 25y = -10$$
$$- (-10x + 6y = 8)$$
$$\overline{19y = -18}$$

$$\frac{19y}{19} = \frac{-18}{19}$$

$$y = -\frac{18}{19}$$

$$2x - 5y = 2$$

$$2x - 5\left(-\frac{18}{19}\right) = 2$$

$$2x + \frac{90}{19} = 2$$

$$2x + \frac{90}{19} - \frac{90}{19} = 2 - \frac{90}{19}$$

$$2x = \frac{38}{19} - \frac{90}{19}$$

$$2x = \frac{-52}{19}$$

$$\frac{2x}{2} = \frac{-52}{19} \div 2$$

$$x = -\frac{26}{19}$$

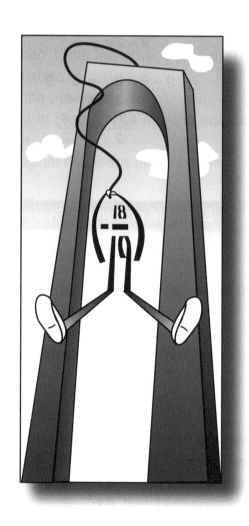

Chapter 3: Linear Equations and Inequalities (cont.)

Example of Solving Linear Equations by Substitution:

$$x - y = 3 \qquad 2x + y = 12$$

$$x - y = 3$$
$$x - y + y = 3 + y$$
$$x = 3 + y$$

$$2x + y = 12$$
$$2(3 + y) + y = 12$$

$$6 + 2y + y = 12$$
$$6 + 3y = 12$$
$$6 - 6 + 3y = 12 - 6$$
$$3y = 6$$

$$\frac{3y}{3} = \frac{6}{3}$$
$$y = 2$$

$$x - y = 3$$
$$x - 2 = 3$$
$$x - 2 + 2 = 3 + 2$$
$$x = 5$$

Name: _____ Date: _____

Chapter 3: Linear Equations and Inequalities (cont.)

Practice: Linear Systems

Directions: Solve the systems of equations. Work the problems on your own paper.

1. $y = -2x + 12$ and $y = 3x - 23$ _____

2. $2x + 3y = 13$ and $3x + 2y = 12$ _____

3. $x - 2y = 9$ and $2x + y = 28$ _____

4. $x + y = 11$ and $x - y = 5$ _____

5. $x + y = 11$ and $x = y - 5$ _____

6. $9 - x = 8$ and $3x + 5y = 28$ _____

7. $3x + y = 13$ and $x - 2y = 2$ _____

8. $13x + 2y = 19$ and $20x - 5y = 5$ _____

9. $x + y = 0$ and $3x + 5y = 10$ _____

10. $5x + 6y = -11$ and $2x - 3y = 1$ _____

11. $2x - y = 1$ and $3x - 2y = -2$ _____

12. $x + 17y = 92$ and $x - 0.5y = 92$ _____

Challenge Problems: Linear Systems

Directions: Work these problems on your own paper.

1. Solve the system of equations. $3x + 7y = 19$ and $3x + 7y = 22$ _____

2. Solve the system of equations. $14x - 5y = 4.5$ and $3y + 3x = 3$ _____

3. Solve the system of equations. $3x + 18y = 22$ and $1.5x + 9y = 11$ _____

Name: _____ Date: _____

Chapter 3: Linear Equations and Inequalities (cont.)

Checking Progress: Linear Equations and Inequalities

1. Find the *y* values for the corresponding *x* values for the linear equation $y = -3 + 2x$.

x	y
-2	
-1	
0	
1	
2	
5	
12	

2. Find the *y* values for the corresponding *x* values for the linear equation $y = 5 - 3x$.

x	y
-2	
-1	
0	
1	
2	
5	
12	

3. Find the *x* values for the corresponding *y* values for the linear equation. $y = 2x + 14$

x	y
	-5
	-2
	0
	1
	100

Directions: Complete the following on your own graph paper or notebook paper.

4. Graph the equation. $y = -0.5x + 5$

5. Graph the equation. $y = 5 - 3x$

6. Graph the inequality. $y < 5x + 7$

7. Graph the inequality. $y \geq -3x + 4$

8. Julian told Erin that the point (-4, 17) was a point on the line $20x + 3y = -29$ and challenged her to find another point. Within 10 seconds, using only mental arithmetic, Erin correctly gave Julian 5 points on the line. List several more points with integer coefficients on the line.

9. Solve the system of equations. $y = 2x - 1$ and $y = 5x - 10$ _____

10. Solve the system of equations. $y = -2x + 1$ and $y = 4x + 7$ _____

Name: _____ Date: _____

Chapter 4: Polynomial Products and Factors

Basic Overview: Simplifying Polynomials and Laws of Exponents

To simplify polynomial expressions, combine like terms. To add or subtract polynomials, first use the distributive property to eliminate parentheses by multiplying each term inside the parentheses by the coefficient, and then combine like terms. Note that for subtraction, the coefficient is -1. This means each term inside the polynomial being subtracted will change sign when the parentheses are removed.

When multiplying two monomials, first multiply their coefficients and then use the product rule of exponents for factors with the same base. Recall that for real numbers, a and b, and positive integers, n and m, the **Laws of Exponents** include:
(1) $a^m \cdot a^n = a^{m+n}$,   (2) $(ab)^m = a^m \cdot b^m$,   and   (3) $(a^m)^n = a^{mn}$.

Examples of Simplifying Polynomials and Laws of Exponents

Example of Simplifying Polynomial Expressions:

$x - 3x^2 + 6 + x^2 - 1 + 4x$
$(-3x^2 + x^2) + (x + 4x) + (6 - 1)$
$-2x^2 + 5x + 5$
This polynomial is simplified, and the degree of the polynomial is 2.

Example of Adding Polynomial Expressions:

Add $3x^2 + 6x - 5$ and $3x^3 + 2x^2 + 4x - 1$

$(3x^2 + 6x - 5) + (3x^3 + 2x^2 + 4x - 1) = 3x^3 + 5x^2 + 10x - 6$
or
$3x^3 + 2x^2 + 4x - 1$
$+ \quad\quad 3x^2 + 6x - 5$
$\overline{3x^3 + 5x^2 + 10x - 6}$

Example of Subtracting Polynomial Expressions:

Subtract $3x^2 + 6x - 5$ from $3x^3 + 2x^2 + 4x - 1$
$(3x^3 + 2x^2 + 4x - 1) - (3x^2 + 6x - 5) = (3x^3 + 2x^2 + 4x - 1) + (-3x^2 - 6x + 5)$
$= 3x^3 + 2x^2 + 4x - 1 - 3x^2 - 6x + 5 = 3x^3 - x^2 - 2x + 4$
or
$3x^3 + 2x^2 + 4x - 1$
$+ \quad\quad -3x^2 - 6x + 5$ Note: All signs changed for the second polynomial.
$\overline{3x^3 - x^2 - 2x + 4}$

Name: _____   Date: _____

Chapter 4: Polynomial Products and Factors (cont.)

Example of The First Law of Exponents, $a^m \cdot a^n = a^{m+n}$:

$$x^2 \cdot x^3 = x^{2+3} = x^5$$

Example of the Second Law of Exponents, $(ab)^m = a^m b^m$:

$$(xy)^2 = x^2 y^2$$

Example of the Third Law of Exponents, $(a^m)^n = a^{mn}$:

$$(c^2)^3 = c^{2(3)} = c^6$$

Examples of Multiplying Polynomials Using the Distributive Property:

$$3(x + 7) = 3 \cdot x + 3 \cdot 7 = 3x + 21$$
$$b(b + 1) = b \cdot b + b \cdot 1 = b^2 + b$$

Practice: Simplifying Polynomials and Laws of Exponents

Directions: Simplify the following.

1. $3x^2 + 4x - 9 + 7x + 3 - 5x^2$ _____

2. $13x^2 - 4x - 19 + 7x^2 + 30 - 5x^2$ _____

3. $3x^3 + 4x^2 - 3 + 7x + 3x - 2x^3 + 4x - 9 + 7x^3$ _____

4. $x^3 - 14x^2 - 3x + 7x^2 + 11x - 2x^3 + 4x$ _____

5. $3x^3 + 4x^2 - 3 + 7x + 3x - (2x^3 + 4x - 9 + 7x^3)$ _____

6. $3x^3 + 4x^2 - [3 + 7x + 3x - (2x^3 + 4x - 9 + 7x^3)]$ _____

7. $4x^3 - 14x^2 + 17x^2 + 11x - 2x^3 + 12x^3 - 14x^2 + 7x^2 + 11 + 4x$ _____

8. $17x^2 + 9x - 2x^3 + 12x^2 - 14x^3 - (4x^2 - 3)$ _____

9. $4x^3 - 14x^2 - (11x - 2x^3) - (\text{-}3 + 7x)$ _____

10. $(2x^3 - 4x^2 + 5x - 6) + (\text{-}5x^3 - 6x^2 - 9x - 11)$ _____

11. $(2x^3 - 4x^2 + 5x - 6) - (\text{-}5x^3 - 6x^2 - 9x - 11)$ _____

Name: _____ Date: _____

Chapter 4: Polynomial Products and Factors (cont.)

12. $(7x^3 - 2x^2 + 14x - 5) - (7x^3 + 2x^2 + 14x + 5)$ _____

13. $3x^3 + 4x^2 - 13x + 0.9 - 0.7x^3 + 2.3x^2 + 1.4x - 0.5$ _____

14. $1.1x^3 + 1.1x^2 + 1.1x + 1.1 - (0.2x^3 + 2.2x^2 + 4.1x - 1.5)$ _____

15. If $2.4x^3 + 6x^2 + 1.6x + 0.75 + b = 1.8x^3 + 6x^2 - 11x + 0.4$, then $b = ?$ _____

Directions: Use the Laws of Exponents to simplify the following problems. Assume that variable exponents are positive integers.

16. $(3a^2)(2a)^2$ _____

17. $(3a)^2(2a^2)$ _____

18. $(3a)^2(2a)^2$ _____

19. $(3ab^2)(2b)^2(a^2b)^3$ _____

20. $(3^2a^2)^2(5a^2)$ _____

21. $(0.5ab^2)(2a^2)^3$ _____

22. $(3a^2bc^3)^3$ _____

23. $[(0.3ab^2)^3]^2$ _____

24. $[2(a^2)(2a)^2]^2$ _____

25. $(3abcd)(2abcd^2)^2$ _____

Challenge Problems: Simplifying Polynomials and Laws of Exponents

1. $7(7x^3 + 2x^2 + 14x + 5) - 5(7x^3 + 2x^2 + 14x + 5) - (7x^3 + 2x^2 + 14x + 5)$ _____

2. $(7x^3 + 2x^2 + 14x + 5) - (6x^3 + 2x^2 + 13x + 4)$ _____

3. If $2.4x^3 + 6x^2 + 1.6x + 0.75 - b = 1.8x^3 + 6x^2 - 11x + 0.4$, then $b = ?$ _____

4. If $18a^4 \div b = 6a^3$, then $b = ?$ _____

5. $[(3a^4)^2]^2$ _____

48

Chapter 4: Polynomial Products and Factors (cont.)

Basic Overview: Multiplying and Factoring Polynomials

To multiply a polynomial by a polynomial, use the distributive property and multiply each term of one polynomial by the other monomial. Whenever two polynomials are multiplied, each term in the first polynomial must be multiplied by every term in the second polynomial, and then like terms are combined. This multiplication process can be simplified by placing the two polynomials in a vertical position, the larger above the smaller. The individual products of monomial times monomial can then be performed, and each result can be placed in an appropriate column for the combining of like terms.

A common method used to multiply two binomials is called the **FOIL method** as follows: (1) multiply both **F**irst terms, then (2) multiply both **O**uter terms, then (3) multiply both **I**nner terms, and finally, (4) multiply both **L**ast terms. The FOIL method is not actually a different method, but rather a way to help students remember to correctly apply the distributive property. Special binomial products that are helpful to memorize include the following:

$(a + b)^2 = (a + b)(a + b) = a^2 + 2ab + b^2$ Square of a sum
$(a - b)^2 = (a - b)(a - b) = a^2 - 2ab + b^2$ Square of a difference
$(a + b)(a - b) = a^2 - b^2$ Product of a sum and a difference

The first step in the factoring of polynomials always involves finding the **greatest common factor (GCF)** for all of the terms. Factoring can then proceed by recognizing special products or by the grouping of terms. The first two trinomials above are called perfect square trinomials, because they can be factored by proceeding from right to left, that is, in the opposite direction of the distributive property as applied under multiplication.

With the third product above, two other binomials that have special factors are as follows:

$a^3 + b^3 = (a + b)(a^2 - ab + b^2)$ Sum of cubes
$a^3 - b^3 = (a - b)(a^2 + ab + b^2)$ Difference of cubes
$a^2 - b^2 = (a + b)(a - b)$ Difference of squares

Example of Multiplying and Factoring Polynomials

Example of Multiplying Polynomials:

$(3x + 2) \bullet (x^2 + 2x - 3)$
$3x \bullet (x^2 + 2x - 3) + 2 \bullet (x^2 + 2x - 3)$
$3x \bullet (x^2) + 3x \bullet (2x) + 3x \bullet (-3) + 2 \bullet (x^2) + 2 \bullet (2x) + 2 \bullet (-3)$
$3x^3 + 6x^2 - 9x + 2x^2 + 4x - 6$
$3x^3 + 8x^2 - 5x - 6$

Name: _____ Date: _____

Chapter 4: Polynomial Products and Factors (cont.)

Example of Factoring Polynomials (GCF):

$2x^4 - 4x^3 + 8x^2$
GCF = $2x^2$
$2x^2(x^2 - 2x + 4)$
The factors of this polynomial are $2x^2$ and $x^2 - 2x + 4$.

Examples of Factoring Polynomials in More than One Step:

$3z^5 - 48z$ GCF = $3z$
$3z(z^4 - 16)$
$3z[(z^2)^2 - (4)^2]$ Difference of squares
$3z(z^2 + 4)(z^2 - 4)$ $4 = 2^2$
$3z(z^2 + 4)(z + 2)(z - 2)$ Difference of squares again!

$40a^3 - 5$ GCF = 5
$5(8a^3 - 1)$
$5[(2a)^3 - 1^3]$ Difference of Cubes
$5(2a - 1)(4a^2 + 2a + 1)$

Practice: Multiplying and Factoring Polynomials

Directions: Multiply the following polynomials. Use your own paper to work the problems.

1. $(2x - 3)(x - 5)$ _____

2. $(3 - 2x)(5 - x)$ _____

3. $(x - 1)(x^2 + x + 1)$ _____

4. $(x^2 + x + 1)(x^2 - x + 1)$ _____

5. $(x - 2y)^2$ _____

6. $(x - 2y)(x^2 - xy + 2)$ _____

7. $(2x^2 - 13x + 15)(x^2 + 3)$ _____

8. $(x + 1)^3$ _____

Name: _____   Date: _____

Chapter 4: Polynomial Products and Factors (cont.)

Directions: Factor the following polynomials.

9. $9 - x^2$ _____

10. $9x^2 + 12xy + 4y^2$ _____

11. $100x^2 - 49$ _____

12. $x^3 + 64y^3$ _____

13. $16y^2 - 40xy + 25x^2$ _____

14. $x^4 - 2x^2y^2 + y^4$ _____

15. $x^2 + 4$ _____

16. $3 - x - 10x^2$ _____

Challenge Problems: Multiplying and Factoring Polynomials

1. Multiply the following. $(x + y)^3$ _____

2. Multiply and combine. $(x + y)^3 - (x - y)^3$ _____

3. Factor. $x^3 + 1$ _____

4. Factor. $ac + ad + bc + bd$ _____

5. Factor. $x^6 - y^6$ _____

6. Given that $x^4 + 4y^4 = (x^4 + 4x^2y^2 + 4y^4) - 4x^2y^2$, complete the factorization of $x^4 + 4y^4$, by using the difference of squares.

_____

Name: _____ Date: _____

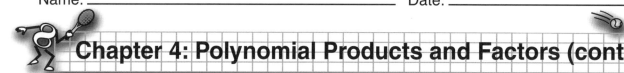

Chapter 4: Polynomial Products and Factors (cont.)

Basic Overview: Solving Polynomial Equations

A **polynomial equation in one variable** is an equation containing the sum of a finite number of terms of the form ax^n, where a is any real number, and n is any whole number. To put a polynomial equation into **standard form** means to put all of the terms on one side of an equation in descending order and set this polynomial expression equal to zero. The solution set for a polynomial equation is the set of all the values of the variable that makes the equation true. These values are called roots, zeros, x-intercepts, and **solutions**.

To find all of the solutions, use factoring methods to rewrite the polynomial expression in standard form as a product of algebraic expressions, normally monomials and binomials. Then set each factor equal to zero and solve for the value of the variable. This procedure utilizes the **zero-factor property**, namely: If A and B are algebraic expressions such that $A \bullet B = 0$, then either $A = 0$ or $B = 0$.

Mathematical models representing real-life situations or problem statements often utilize polynomial equations.

Example of Mathematical Model Using a Polynomial Equation:

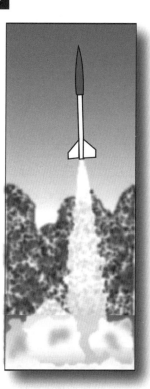

A rocket is shot upward at the velocity of 96 ft./sec. How long is the rocket in the air before it lands?

The height of the rocket above ground level can be considered as a function of the time. This function can be written as $h(t) = v \bullet t - 16 \bullet t^2$, where h is the height in feet, t is the time in seconds, and v is the initial velocity.

The height at launch and landing is $h = 0$, so the solutions to the polynomial equation $96t - 16t^2 = 0$ need to be determined.

$96t - 16t^2 = 0$ GCF $= 16t$

$16t(6 - t) = 0$ Apply zero-factor property.

       $16t = 0$ or $6 - t = 0$

       $\dfrac{16t}{16} = \dfrac{0}{16}$ $6 - t + t = 0 + t$

         $t = 0$ $6 = t$

The rocket was in the air for 6 seconds.

Name: _____ Date: _____

Chapter 4: Polynomial Products and Factors (cont.)

Practice: Solving Polynomial Equations

Directions: Solve the following equations. Use your own paper to work the problems.

1. $x^2 - 12 = x$ _____

2. $x^2 + 7x + 10 = 0$ _____

3. $2x^2 + 13x - 7 = 0$ _____

4. $15x^2 + 7x - 2 = 0$ _____

5. $x^2 + 5x + 13 = 0$ _____

6. $25x^2 - 20x + 4 = 0$ _____

7. $25x^2 - 4 = 0$ _____

8. Find a quadratic equation that has $x = 1$ and $x = 2$ as solutions.

   _____

9. A number of coins can be placed in a square array with 15 coins on a side. It can also be arranged in a rectangular array with 16 more coins in the length than in the width. How many coins are on the length and width of the rectangular array?

   _____

10. Find two consecutive even integers whose product is 728.

   _____

Challenge Problems: Solving Polynomial Equations

Directions: Use your own paper to work the problems.

1. $y^2 = y + 12$ _____

2. $x^2 = x + 30$ _____

Chapter 4: Polynomial Products and Factors (cont.)

Checking Progress: Polynomial Products and Factors

1. Simplify. $5x^3 - 4x^2 - 3 - 3x - (-2x^3 + 4x - 9 + 7x^2)$ _____

2. If $b - (2.4x^3 - 6x^2 - 1.6x + 0.75) = 1.8x^3 + 6x^2 + x + 0.4$, then $b = ?$ _____

3. Simplify. $(0.4a^2b^5)^3$ _____

4. Simplify. $(ab^2)(2a)^3(a^2)^{10}$ _____

5. Multiply. $(2x + 1)^3$ _____

6. Multiply. $(x + 2y)(x^2 + xy)$ _____

7. Factor. $9x^2 - 6x - 35$ _____

8. Factor. $64x^3 + y^3$ _____

9. Solve. $20x^2 + 23x + 12 = 0$ _____

10. The altitude of a triangle is 8 inches less than its base. What are the base and altitude of the triangle if the area of the triangle is 640 square inches?

    _____

Name: _____ Date: _____

Chapter 5: Rational Expressions

Basic Overview: Rational Expressions

A **rational expression** (also called an algebraic fraction) is a ratio of two polynomials in which the denominator is not the zero polynomial, that is, the number zero. Because division by zero is undefined, we always assume that the value or values of the variable that make the denominator of a rational expression equal to zero are also excluded. A rational expression is said to be reduced to its lowest terms when the numerator and the denominator contain no common factors other than 1.

The multiplication of rational expressions proceeds in the same manner as the multiplication of rational numbers, that is, $\frac{a}{b} \cdot \frac{c}{d} = \frac{a \cdot c}{b \cdot d}$. Any common factor can be divided out as is done when simplifying rational expressions. Remember the **basic principle of rational numbers** $\left(\frac{a}{b} = \frac{ac}{bc}, c \neq 0\right)$ states that every rational number or expression has infinitely many equivalent forms.

The division of rational expressions is defined by multiplication as follows: $\frac{a}{b} \div \frac{m}{n} = \frac{a}{b} \cdot \frac{n}{m}$, that is, invert the divisor (the second fraction) and multiply.

Recall that fractions can only be added or subtracted if their denominators are identical, both illustrated as follows: $\frac{a}{b} + \frac{c}{b} = \frac{a + c}{b}$ and $\frac{a}{b} - \frac{c}{b} = \frac{a - c}{b}$.

To add or subtract fractions with different denominators, we must first find a common denominator, which is usually the **least common multiple (LCM)** of all of the denominators involved. This multiple is called the **least common denominator (LCD)**. Use the following steps to find the LCD:

(1) Factor each denominator completely.

(2) Write a product that contains each factor that appears in any denominator.

(3) When a factor appears more than once, use the highest power that does appear.

Now, rewrite each fraction as an equivalent fraction with the LCD as the denominator. Add or subtract the numerators of the equivalent fractions, as appropriate. To finish, reduce the resulting fraction to its lowest terms.

When simplifying fractions, you can use the following two concepts to assist you:

(1) There are three signs associated with every fraction, namely, the sign of the numerator, the sign of the denominator, and the sign of the fraction itself. This means that two of the signs can be changed, and the value of the fraction remains unchanged as follows: $\frac{-a}{b} = -\frac{a}{b} = \frac{a}{-b}$ ·(2) Any two binomials of the form, $(a - b)$ and $(b - a)$, are called opposites because $(a - b) = -(b - a)$, and vice versa. When dividing opposites, the quotient is always equal to -1.

Name: _____ Date: _____

Chapter 5: Rational Expressions (cont.)

Challenge Problems: Rational Expressions

Directions: Work the following problems on your own paper, and then write the answers on the blanks provided.

1. Write the following in scientific notation: $(1.2 \cdot 10^4) \cdot (12 \cdot 10^4)$ _____

2. Write the following in decimal form: $0.0012 \cdot 10^{-4}$ _____

3. Tara thought that 3^{2^3} was the same as 3^{3^2}. Wendy didn't think they were the same. With whom do you agree and why?

   _____

   _____

4. Simplify. $\dfrac{2^{3^2}}{2^{4^2}}$ _____

5. Simplify into one fraction. $\dfrac{2}{3}x + \dfrac{5}{7}y - \dfrac{1}{2}z$ _____

6. Simplify. $\dfrac{3}{(x-4)(x+3)} + \dfrac{5}{(x-2)(x-4)}$ _____

7. Solve. $\left(\dfrac{x+1}{x-1}\right)^2 + \left(\dfrac{x+1}{x-1}\right) - 2 = 0$ _____

8. What number added to the numerators and denominators of both fractions $\dfrac{2}{3}$ and $\dfrac{5}{8}$ makes the resulting fractions have the same value?

   _____

Name: _____ Date: _____

Chapter 5: Rational Expressions (cont.)

Checking Progress: Rational Expressions

Directions: Work the problems on your own paper, and write the answers on the blanks provided.

1. Simplify. $\dfrac{(8x)^3 \cdot 18y^{12}}{(3x^2)^2 \cdot (2y^2)^4}$ _____

2. If $\left(\dfrac{2^4 \cdot 3^6 \cdot 5^{41}}{7^3 \cdot 11^4}\right)(b) = \dfrac{2^3 \cdot 3^7 \cdot 7^3}{5^3 \cdot 11}$, then $b =$? _____

3. Write in scientific notation. 0.002352 _____

4. Write in decimal form. $6.02 \cdot 10^5$ _____

5. Simplify. $\dfrac{(5x)^4}{3(xy^2)^2} \cdot \dfrac{(2y)^3}{20x^2y}$

   _____

6. Simplify. $\dfrac{(x-2)}{3(x+5)} + \dfrac{(x+7)}{7(x+2)}$

   _____

7. Solve. $\dfrac{60}{x} - \dfrac{60}{x-5} = \dfrac{2}{x}$

   _____

8. Solve. $\dfrac{2x+3}{x-1} = \dfrac{10}{x^2-1} = \dfrac{2x-3}{x+1}$

   _____

9. Simplify into one fraction. $\dfrac{2}{5}x - \dfrac{3}{7}y + \dfrac{1}{3}z$ _____

10. In a rational number, the numerator is 3 more than the denominator. If 2 is added to both the denominator and numerator, the result is $\dfrac{3}{2}$. What is the rational number?

    _____

Name: _____ Date: _____

Chapter 6: Roots, Radicals, and Complex Numbers (cont.)

Example of Multiplying the Numerator and Denominator of a Radical Expression by the Same Number:

$$\frac{5}{\sqrt{3}} =$$

$$\frac{5}{\sqrt{3}}\left(\frac{\sqrt{3}}{\sqrt{3}}\right) =$$

$$\frac{5\sqrt{3}}{\sqrt{3(3)}} = \frac{5\sqrt{3}}{\sqrt{9}} = \frac{5\sqrt{3}}{3}$$

$$\frac{5}{\sqrt{3}} = \frac{5\sqrt{3}}{3}$$

Example of Radical Expressions Added and Subtracted if Each Index Is the Same and Each Radicand Is the Same:

$$2\sqrt[3]{17} + \sqrt[3]{17} =$$

$$(2+1) \bullet \sqrt[3]{17} = 3\sqrt[3]{17}$$

Example of Radical Expressions Written as Fractional Exponents:

$$\sqrt[4]{x^3} = (x^3)^{\frac{1}{4}} = x^{\frac{3}{4}}$$

Example of Changing Fractional Exponents Into Radical Expressions:

$$y^{\frac{5}{3}} = (y^5)^{\frac{1}{3}} = \sqrt[3]{y^5} = \sqrt[3]{y^3 \bullet y^2} = \sqrt[3]{y^3} \bullet \sqrt[3]{y^2} = y \bullet \sqrt[3]{y^2}$$

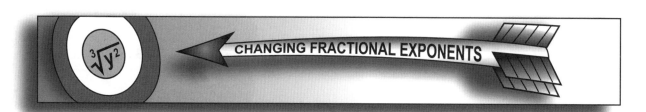

CHANGING FRACTIONAL EXPONENTS

Name: _____   Date: _____

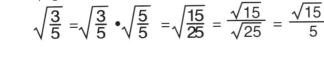

Chapter 6: Roots, Radicals, and Complex Numbers (cont.)

Example of Rationalizing the Denominator:

$$\sqrt{\frac{3}{5}}$$

$$\sqrt{\frac{3}{5}} = \sqrt{\frac{3}{5}} \cdot \sqrt{\frac{5}{5}} = \sqrt{\frac{15}{25}} = \frac{\sqrt{15}}{\sqrt{25}} = \frac{\sqrt{15}}{5}$$

Example of Simplifying Like Radicals:

$$\sqrt{8} + \sqrt{98}$$

$$\sqrt{8} + \sqrt{98} = \sqrt{2 \cdot 4} + \sqrt{2 \cdot 49} = 2\sqrt{2} + 7\sqrt{2} = 9\sqrt{2}$$

Practice: Simplifying Radicals, Products, Quotients, Sums, Differences

Directions: Simplify the following. Use your own paper to work the problems.

1. $\sqrt[3]{a^3}$ _____

2. $\sqrt[4]{2^4 a^4}$ _____

3. $\sqrt[4]{32}$ _____

4. $\sqrt[3]{250a^7}$ _____

5. $\sqrt[3]{\dfrac{a^2 b^4}{27}}$ _____

6. $\sqrt[5]{\dfrac{b^{10}}{16y^5}}$ _____

7. $\sqrt{32} + \sqrt{50}$ _____

8. $2\sqrt{75} - \sqrt{48}$ _____

9. $3\sqrt[3]{5} - \sqrt[3]{40}$ _____

10. $\sqrt{27} - \sqrt{\dfrac{1}{3}}$ _____

11. $\sqrt{\dfrac{1}{2}} - \sqrt{\dfrac{1}{8}}$ _____

12. $\sqrt[4]{\dfrac{9}{8}} - \sqrt[4]{\dfrac{2}{9}}$ _____

13. $\sqrt{c} - 4\sqrt{c} + \sqrt{c}$

_____

14. $10\sqrt{\dfrac{3}{5}} + 30\sqrt{\dfrac{5}{3}}$

_____

Name: _____   Date: _____

Chapter 6: Roots, Radicals, and Complex Numbers (cont.)

Basic Overview: Simplifying Binomials With Radicals and Solving Radical Equations

Binomial expressions containing radicals can be multiplied just like binomials were multiplied using the FOIL method or using the distributive property twice to eliminate one set of parentheses. Both methods are shown in the examples below.

To solve equations containing radical expressions: (1) Use algebraic rules of equality to isolate the radical on one side of the equation; (2) Next, square both sides of the equation if the radical is a square root, or cube both sides if the radical is a cube root; (3) Then solve the resulting equation; and (4) Finally, check your answer(s) in the original equation since this procedure can produce **extraneous solutions**.

When solving a linear equation that contains radicals as coefficients and/or constants, it is not necessary to square both sides of the equation. Apply the algebraic rules of equality along with the rules for simplifying radical expressions.

Examples of Simplifying Binomials With Radicals and Solving Radical Equations

Example of Multiplying Binomials With Radicals:

$$\left(4 + \sqrt{7}\right)\left(3 + 2\sqrt{7}\right)$$
$$4\left(3 + 2\sqrt{7}\right) + \sqrt{7}\left(3 + 2\sqrt{7}\right)$$
$$12 + 8\sqrt{7} + 3\sqrt{7} + 2\left(\sqrt{7}\right)^2$$
$$12 + 11\sqrt{7} + 2(7)$$
$$12 + 11\sqrt{7} + 14$$
$$26 + 11\sqrt{7}$$

Example of Solving Radical Equations With Square Roots:

$$\sqrt{2x - 1} = 3$$
$$\left(\sqrt{2x - 1}\right)^2 = 3^2$$
$$2x - 1 = 9$$
$$2x - 1 + 1 = 9 + 1$$
$$2x = 10$$
$$\frac{2x}{2} = \frac{10}{2}$$
$$x = 5$$

Name: _____ Date: _____

Chapter 6: Roots, Radicals, and Complex Numbers (cont.)

Example of Solving Radical Equations With Cube Roots:

$$2\sqrt[3]{x} - 1 = 3$$

$$2\sqrt[3]{x} - 1 + 1 = 3 + 1$$

$$2\sqrt[3]{x} = 4$$

$$\left(2\sqrt[3]{x}\right)^3 = 4^3$$

$$8x = 64$$

$$\frac{8x}{8} = \frac{64}{8}$$

$$x = 8$$

Example of Solving a Linear Equation With a Radical:

$$3x = 2 + x\sqrt{5}$$

$$3x - x\sqrt{5} = 2 + x\sqrt{5} - x\sqrt{5}$$

$$x\left(3 - \sqrt{5}\right) = 2$$

$$\frac{x\left(3 - \sqrt{5}\right)}{3 - \sqrt{5}} = \frac{2}{3 - \sqrt{5}}$$

$$x = \frac{2}{3 - \sqrt{5}}$$

$$x = \frac{2}{3 - \sqrt{5}} \cdot \frac{3 + \sqrt{5}}{3 + \sqrt{5}}$$

$$x = \frac{2\left(3 + \sqrt{5}\right)}{9 - 5}$$

$$x = \frac{6 + 2\sqrt{5}}{4}$$

$$x = \frac{3 + \sqrt{5}}{2}$$

Chapter 6: Roots, Radicals, and Complex Numbers (cont.)

Directions: Simplify the following complex expressions. Use your own paper to work the problems.

9. $2i - (4 - 3i)$ _____

10. $(-2 + 8i) - (7 + 3i)$ _____

11. $(4 - 2i) - (5 - 3i)$ _____

12. $(9i)^2$ _____

13. $(5 - 2i)^2$ _____

14. $(3 + 2i)(1 + i)$ _____

15. $(4 + 3i)(2 + i)$ _____

16. $(1 + i)(1 - i)$ _____

17. $\dfrac{3 + 2i}{2 + i}$ _____

18. $\dfrac{5 - 10i}{-3 + 4i}$ _____

19. $\dfrac{3 - 2i}{2 - i}$ _____

20. $\dfrac{4 - 2i}{4 + 2i}$ _____

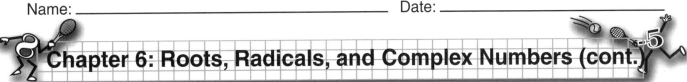

Chapter 6: Roots, Radicals, and Complex Numbers (cont.)

Challenge Problems: Decimal Representation and Complex Numbers

1. Write $\frac{1}{19}$ in decimal notation. _____

2. What fraction, with whole numbers for the numerator and denominator, is equivalent to $0.\overline{571428}$? _____

3. When asked to write $\frac{7}{99}$ in decimal form, Linda used her calculator. She wrote what her display showed, 0.070707071. Was Linda correct? Why or why not? _____

_____

_____

4. Neelie and Stewart were trying to determine another way to write the number 0.999999999999…….. They finally concluded that this was just another way to write the number 1. Do you agree with them? Why or why not? _____

_____

_____

_____

5. Simplify. $\dfrac{1 + i}{(1 - i)^2}$ _____

6. Simplify. $(3 + i\sqrt{2})(3 - i\sqrt{2})$ _____

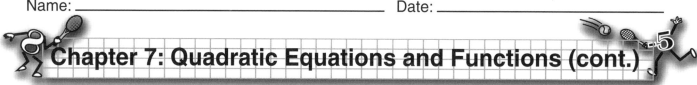

Chapter 7: Quadratic Equations and Functions (cont.)

Example of Putting a Quadratic Equation Into Standard Form:

$a(2a + 8) = 10$

$(a \cdot 2a) + (a \cdot 8) = 10$ Distributive Property

$(2a^2 + 8a) - 10 = 10 - 10$ Addition Property of Equality

$2a^2 + 8a - 10 = 0$ Standard form, ready to solve

Example of Putting a Quadratic Equation Into Standard Form:

$(y - 5)(y - 3) = 8$

$y^2 - 3y - 5y + 15 = 8$ FOIL method

$y^2 - 8y + 15 = 8$ Combine like terms.

$y^2 - 8y + 15 - 8 = 8 - 8$ Subtraction Property of Equality

$y^2 - 8y + 7 = 0$ Standard form, ready to solve

Example of Putting a Quadratic Equation Into Standard Form:

$3x^2 - 7x = 4$

$3x^2 - 7x - 4 = 4 - 4$ Subtraction Property of Equality

$3x^2 - 7x - 4 = 0$ Standard form, ready to solve

Example of Solving a Quadratic Equation of the Form, $ax^2 + c = 0$:

$2x^2 - 98 = 0$

$(2x^2 - 98) + 98 = 0 + 98$ Addition Property of Equality

$2x^2 + (\text{-}98 + 98) = 98$ Associate Property of Addition

$2x^2 = 98$

$\frac{1}{2} \cdot 2x^2 = \frac{1}{2} \cdot 98$ Multiplication Property of Equality

$x^2 = 49$ Square Root Property

$x = \pm \sqrt{49} = \pm 7$

Name: _____   Date: _____

Chapter 7: Quadratic Equations and Functions (cont.)

Example of Solving a Quadratic Equation of the Form, $ax^2 + bx = 0$:

$x^2 + 10x = 0$ Factor an x from both terms on the left side.

$x \cdot (x + 10) = 0$ Use the Zero-Product Property,

Set both factors on the left side equal to zero and solve each linear equation:

$x = 0$ or $x + 10 = 0$

$(x + 10) - 10 = 0 - 10$

$x + (10 - 10) = \text{-}10$

$x = 0$ or $x = \text{-}10$

Example of Using the Factoring Method to Solve a Quadratic Equation of the Form, $ax^2 + bx + c = 0$:

$x^2 - 5x + 4 = 0$ Determine the two numbers whose sum is -5 and whose product is +4. The two numbers are -1 and -4.

$x^2 - 4x - 1x + 4 = 0$ Rewrite the middle term -5x as $-4x - 1x$.

$x \cdot (x - 4) - 1 \cdot (x - 4) = 0$ Factor the four terms by grouping each set of two terms.

$(x - 4) \cdot (x - 1) = 0$ Use the Zero-Product Property to solve by setting each linear factor equal to zero.

$x - 1 = 0$ or $x - 4 = 0$

$(x - 1) + 1 = 0 + 1$ $(x - 4) + 4 = 0 + 4$

$x + (\text{-}1 + 1) = 1$ $x + (\text{-}4 + 4) = 4$

$x = 1$ or $x = 4$

Name: _____   Date: _____

Chapter 7: Quadratic Equations and Functions (cont.)

Example of the Completing the Square Method to Solve a Quadratic Equation:

$x^2 + 2x = 1$

$x^2 + 2x + 1 = 1 + 1$ Make it look like a perfect square by adding 1 to both sides.

$x^2 + 2x + 1 = 2$

$(x + 1)^2 = 2$ Factor the equation.

$\sqrt{(x + 1)^2} = \pm\sqrt{2}$ The solution can be found by taking the square root of each side.

$x + 1 = \pm\sqrt{2}$

$(x + 1) - 1 = \left(\pm\sqrt{2}\right) - 1$

$x = -1 \pm \sqrt{2}$

$x = -1 + \sqrt{2}$ or $x = -1 - \sqrt{2}$ are the two solutions for the equation.

Example of Determining the Nature of the Roots:

$3x^2 - 7x + 5 = 0$

$D = b^2 - 4ac$

$D = (-7)^2 - 4(3)(5)$

$D = 49 - 60$

$D = -11$

A negative value for D indicates that the roots are complex conjugates.

Chapter 7: Quadratic Equations and Functions (cont.)

Practice: Solving Quadratic Equations

Directions: Form a quadratic equation from a linear equation by the variable in the equation.

1. $4x(x + 1) = 0$ _____

2. $-5x(3x + 4) = 0$ _____

3. $\frac{1}{2}x\left(\frac{2}{3} - x\right) = 0$ _____

4. $0.2x(5x - 1) = -2$ _____

5. $-3x(4 - 2x) = -4$ _____

6. $7a(a + 9) = -8$ _____

7. $-t(-t - 1) = -1$ _____

8. $(-3s + 5)^2 - 4s = -7$ _____

9. $15x\left(\frac{1}{5}x + \frac{2}{3}\right) = -3$ _____

10. $20t(0.25t - 0.75) = 1.5$ _____

Directions: Form a quadratic equation by multiplying binomial expressions.

11. $(x + 2)(x - 3) = 0$ _____

12. $(2x - 1)(x - 5) = 0$ _____

13. $(3s - 2)(4s + 3) = 0$ _____

14. $(t - 7)(t - 5) = 0$ _____

15. $(2c + 3)(5c - 7) = 0$ _____

16. $(3x + 5)(8x + 13) = 0$ _____

17. $(s - 4)(s + 9) = 0$ _____

18. $(5s - 2)(2s - 5) = 0$ _____

19. $(x - 7)(2x + 1) = 0$ _____

20. $(3t + 3)(4t + 4) = 0$ _____

Name: _____ Date: _____

Chapter 7: Quadratic Equations and Functions (cont.)

Directions: Use factoring to solve. Work the problem on your own paper if you need more room.

21. $4z^2 + 28z + 49 = 0$ _____

22. $x^2 - 5x + 6 = 0$ _____

23. $x^2 - 3x - 10 = 0$ _____

24. $10t^2 - 7t - 12 = 0$ _____

25. $15x^2 + 4x - 3 = 0$ _____

26. $2 + 5x - 12x^2 = 0$ _____

27. $12x^2 = 12 - 32x$ _____

28. $6b^2 + 19b - 7 = 0$ _____

29. $4x^2 - 8x = 0$ _____

30. $81 - 4x^2 = 0$ _____

Directions: Use the complete the square method to solve. Work the problem on your own paper if you need more room.

31. $x^2 - 4x - 3 = 0$ _____

32. $x^2 - 10x + 21 = 0$ _____

33. $x^2 + 6x + 7 = 0$ _____

Directions: Use the quadratic formula to solve. Work the problem on your own paper if you need more room.

34. $x^2 - 2x - 6 = 0$ _____

35. $9x^2 + 6x - 4 = 0$ _____

36. $-15x^2 - 10x + 25 = 0$ _____

37. $3x - 2x^2 = 4 - 5x^2$ _____

38. $3x^2 - 2x - 1 = 0$ _____

39. $7x^2 = 3 - 5x$ _____

Chapter 7: Quadratic Equations and Functions (cont.)

Directions: Solve using a quadratic equation.

40. A rectangle has a length of $x + 1.5$ inches, a width of x inches, and an area of 18.36 square inches. Find its dimensions.

   _____

41. You throw a stone upward from a cliff 61 feet above the ground with an initial velocity of 36 feet per second. The height of the stone at time t is modeled by $h = -16t^2 + 36t + 61$. Find the time when the ball hits the ground below.

   _____

Directions: Without solving, determine the nature of the roots of each quadratic equation.

42. $14x^2 + 11x - 40 = 0$ _____

43. $3x^2 - 13x + 169 = 0$ _____

Chapter 7: Quadratic Equations and Functions (cont.)

Directions: Use the complete the square method to solve.

7. $x^2 + 2x - 8 = 0$ _____

Directions: Use the quadratic formula to solve.

8. $3x^2 - x + 4 = 0$ 9. $-2x^2 + 5x + 3 = 0$

_____   _____

10. Complete the table below.

Function	Parabola Opens Up or Down	Narrow or Wide
A. $f(x) = -x^2 + 2$	_____	_____
B. $g(x) = -3x^2 + 2x + 11$	_____	_____

11. For each quadratic function below, find the vertex for the parabola.

A. $f(x) = -2x^2 + 7x + 9$ _____

B. $f(x) = 3x^2 - 2x + 5$ _____

12. For each quadratic function, find the *x*-intercepts, if they exist.

A. $f(x) = x^2 + 8x - 3$ _____

B. $f(x) = -3x^2 - 9x + 2$ _____

13. Using your own graph paper, graph the function given by $f(x) = x^2 - 2x + 5$.

Name: _____ Date: _____

Chapter 8: Variation

Basic Overview: Direct Variation, Proportion, Inverse Variation, Joint Variation

Certain relationships between two variables can be described by indicating how one variable changes according to the change in values of the second variable.

When two variables both increase or decrease together, they are in **direct variation**. The statement "y varies directly as x or y is directly proportional to x" means that $y = k \cdot x$ for some fixed, non-zero, real number k, that is called the **constant of variation**.

When one variable increases and the second variable decreases, or vice versa, they exhibit **inverse variation**. The statement "y varies inversely as x or y is inversely proportional to x" means that $y = k \cdot \dfrac{1}{x}$ or $y = \dfrac{k}{x}$ for a fixed, non-zero constant of variation, k.

When one variable varies directly as the product of two or more other variables, the first is said to be in **joint variation** with the others. The statement "y varies jointly as x and the square of z or y is jointly proportional to x and the square of z" means that $y = k \cdot xz^2$, once again, for a fixed constant of variation, k.

Combined variation is a combination of both direct and inverse relations. Note that variation formulas never involve addition or subtraction operators.

A **proportion** is a statement that two ratios are equal. Since a statement of direct variation can be written as $\dfrac{y}{x} = k$, then two different sets of values for x and y, that is, two ordered pairs from the direct variation relation, can be set equal: $\dfrac{y_1}{x_1} = \dfrac{y_2}{x_2}$. Cross-multiplication of this proportion yields: $y_1 x_2 = x_1 y_2$, which is referred to as: the product of the means being equal to the product of the extremes. This is always true for a direct proportion, and it allows us to avoid using the constant of variation when comparing any two sets of coordinated values from the direct variation relation. Notice that an inverse variation can be written in the form $x \cdot y = k$. This means that for two ordered pairs of x and y values from the inverse relation, we obtain the following calculating equation: $x_1 y_1 = x_2 y_2$.

Examples of Direct, Inverse, and Joint Variation

Examples of Direct Variation:

Gina works in a department store earning $7.50/hour. The constant is k = hourly wage. x = number of hours, y = amount earned.
$y = \$7.50x \ (k \neq 0)$

# Hours (x)	Hourly Wage (k) constant of variation	Total Earned (y) $y = kx$
1	$7.50	$y = \$7.50(1) = \$7.50$
5	$7.50	$y = \$7.50(5) = \$37.50$
10	$7.50	$y = \$7.50(10) = \$75.00$

95

Name: _____ Date: _____

Chapter 8: Variation (cont.)

Example of Product of Extremes and Means:

If y varies directly as x and $y = 15$ when $x = 24$, find x when $y = 25$.

$x_2 = ?$ $y_2 = 25$ $x_1 = 24$ $y_1 = 15$

$$y_1 x_2 = x_1 y_2$$

$$x_2(15) = 24(25)$$

$$15x_2 = 600$$

$$\frac{15x_2}{15} = \frac{600}{15}$$

$$x_2 = 40$$

Example of Inverse Variation:

If y is inversely proportional to x and $y = 6$ when $x = 5$, find x when $y = 12$.

$$xy = k$$

$$y = \frac{k}{x}$$

$$6 = \frac{k}{5}$$

$$6(5) = \frac{k}{5}(5)$$

$$30 = k \qquad \text{The formula is } y = \frac{30}{x}$$

$$12 = \frac{30}{x}$$

$$12(x) = \frac{30}{x}(x)$$

$$12x = 30$$

$$\frac{12x}{12} = \frac{30}{12} \qquad\qquad x = \frac{30}{12} = \frac{5}{2}$$

Name: _____ Date: _____

Chapter 8: Variation (cont.)

Example of Joint Variation:

If z varies jointly as x and the square root of y, then $z = k(x)(\sqrt{y})$, $(k \neq 0)$, and $z = 6$ when $x = 3$ and $y = 16$, find z when $x = 7$ and $y = 4$.

$z = k(x)(\sqrt{y})$

$6 = k(3)(\sqrt{16})$

$6 = k(3)(4)$

$6 = 12k$

$\dfrac{6}{12} = \dfrac{12k}{12}$

$\dfrac{1}{2} = k$

The equation of the joint variation is $z = \dfrac{1}{2}x\sqrt{y}$.

$z = \dfrac{1}{2}(7)\sqrt{4}$

$z = \dfrac{1}{2}(7)(2)$

$z = \dfrac{1}{2}(14)$

$z = 7$

Name: _____ Date: _____

Chapter 8: Variation (cont.)

Practice: Variation

Directions: Work these problems on your own paper, and write the answers on the lines below.

Direct Variation

1. If *y* varies directly as *x,* and *y* = 10 when *x* = 5, find *x* when *y* = 3. _____

2. If *y* varies directly as *x,* and *y* = 16 when *x* = 10, find *x* when *y* = 15. _____

3. If *y* varies directly as *x,* and *y* = 3 when *x* = 4, find *x* when *y* = 5. _____

4. If *y* varies directly as *x,* and *y* = 14 when *x* = 7, find *y* when *x* = 4. _____

5. If *y* varies directly as *x,* and *y* = 24 when *x* = 4, find *y* when *x* = 12. _____

6. If *y* varies directly as *x,* and *y* = 12 when *x* = 2, find *y* when *x* = 15. _____

7. If *a* is directly proportional to *b,* and *a* = 3 when *b* = 9, find *b* when *a* = 4. _____

8. If *a* is directly proportional to *b,* and *a* = 4 when *b* = 2, find *b* when *a* = 7. _____

9. If *a* is directly proportional to *b,* and *a* = 6 when *b* = 12, find *b* when *a* = 10. _____

Inverse Variation

10. If *y* is inversely proportional to *x,* and *y* = 10 when *x* = 2, find *x* when *y* = 4. _____

11. If *y* is inversely proportional to *x,* and *y* = 2 when *x* = 7, find *x* when *y* = 12. _____

12. If *y* is inversely proportional to *x,* and *y* = 5 when *x* = 3, find *x* when *y* = 2. _____

Joint Variation

13. If *z* is jointly proportional to *x* and *y,* and *z* = 20 when *x* = 10 and *y* = 1, find *z* when *x* = 4 and *y* = 7. _____

14. If *z* is jointly proportional to *x* and *y,* and *z* = 18 when *x* = 2 and *y* = 3, find *z* when *x* = 9 and *y* = 5. _____

Name: _____ Date: _____

Chapter 8: Variation (cont.)

Challenge Problems: Direct Variation

Directions: Work these problems on your own paper, and write the answers on the lines below.

1. If y is inversely proportional to x, and $y = p$ when $x = 5$, find y when $x = 4$. _____

2. If y and z are both inversely proportional to x, and $y = 10$ when $x = 2$, and $z = 10$ when $x = 4$, Jim thought that when $x = 8$, y would be twice as big as z. Was Jim correct?

   _____

3. If y and z are both directly proportional to x, and $y = 10$ when $x = 2$, and $z = 10$ when $x = 4$, Jim thought that when $x = 8$, y would be twice as big as z. Was Jim correct?

   _____

4. If x is directly proportional to y, and y is directly proportional to z, how is x related to z?

   _____

Checking Progress: Variation

Directions: Work these problems on your own paper, and write the answers on the lines below.

1. If y varies directly as x, and $y = 12$ when $x = 6$, find x when $y = 8$. _____

2. If y varies directly as x, and $y = 1.6$ when $x = 10$, find x when $y = 15$. _____

3. If y varies directly as x, and $y = 14$ when $x = 0.7$, find y when $x = 4$. _____

4. If y varies directly as x, and $y = 24$ when $x = 4$, find x when $y = 12$. _____

5. If a is directly proportional to b, and $a = 90$ when $b = 0.3$, find b when $a = 4$. _____

6. If a is directly proportional to b, and $a = 14$ when $b = 2$, find b when $a = 7$. _____

7. If y is inversely proportional to x, and $y = 10$ when $x = 0.2$, find x when $y = 4$. _____

8. If y is inversely proportional to x, and $y = 20$ when $x = 6$, find x when $y = 1.2$. _____

9. If z is jointly proportional to x, and y and $z = 2$ when $x = 10$ and $y = 1$, find z when $x = 4$ and $y = 7$. _____

10. If y is inversely proportional to x, and $y = p$ when $x = 7$, find y when $x = 3.5$. _____

Name: _____ Date: _____

Check-up Problems: Solving Equations and Problems

Directions: Complete the following.

1. Simplify. $13x + 6(2 - x) - 3(x - 2) + 8$ _____

2. Simplify. $131(4 - 2t) - 11(4 - 2t) - 120(4 - 2t)$ _____

3. If $3x + 5(3 - x) + a = 22 - 5x$, then $a = ?$ _____

4. Solve. $12 + 3^2(2 - 3x) = 111$ _____

5. Solve. $2 + [5 - (9 - 2x)] = 7 + 5x$ _____

6. Solve. $43(9 - 3x) + 32(9 - 3x) = 25(3x - 9)$ _____

7. Hamilton High School has 900 students in school. There are 60 more girls than boys. How many boys and how many girls are there?

   _____

8. Natasha has cell phone service from Varisoon Wireless. She pays a flat fee of $39.95 for 350 minutes per month. Any minutes over 350 are at an additional cost. In November, Natasha's bill for wireless service was $107.45 for 575 minutes. What is the charge per minute for minutes over 350 per month?

   _____

9. Laronda is a painter. She charges $400 for the paint plus $12.50 per hour to paint a house. Her bill is $775. How many hours did she work?

   _____

10. Su was to make a triangle with the following conditions. One angle was to be 6° more than double the other with the third being 1° less than one-half of the smaller of the other two. What were the angle measures in the triangle Su made?

    _____

Name: _____ Date: _____

Check-up Problems: Inequalities

Directions: Complete the following.

1. T or F? $12 - 5(2) + 3 > 7 - 9 + 5$

2. T or F? If $x > 0$, $92x + 443 > 2x + 443$

3. Graph on a number line. $b \leq -(9 - 13)$

4. Graph on a number line. $-x + 3 > 3 - 4 + 5$

5. Solve. $-3x + 14 < 18 - 5x$ _____

6. $8(4x - 2) < 16(4x - 2)$ _____

7. $x < 29$ or $x < 3$ _____

8. $-4x + 5 < 9$ or $1 + 2x < 5$ _____

9. $|3x - 7| \geq 14$ _____

10. $\left|\frac{2}{5}x + 3\right| \leq 11$ _____

Name: _____ Date: _____

Check-up Problems: Linear Equations and Inequalities

Directions: Complete the following.

1. Find the *y* values for the corresponding *x* values for the linear equation $y = 5x - 13$.

x	y
-2	
-1	
0	
1	
2	
5	
12	

2. Find the *y* values for the corresponding *x* values for the linear equation $y = 13 - 5x$.

x	y
-2	
-1	
0	
1	
2	
5	
12	

3. Find the *x* values for the corresponding *y* values for the linear equation $y = -x - 4$.

x	y
	-5
	-2
	0
	1
	100

Directions: Use your own graph paper for the following.

4. Graph the equation. $y = -1.5x + 2.5$

5. Graph the equation. $y = \frac{2}{3}x - 2$

Name: _____ Date: _____

Check-up Problems: Linear Equations and Inequalities (cont.)

6. Graph the inequality. $y \geq -5x + 4$

7. Graph the inequality. $y < 9x - 13$

8. Julian told Erin that the point (8, 1) was a point on the line $200x + 9y = 1{,}609$ and challenged her to find another point. Within 10 seconds, using only mental arithmetic, Erin correctly gave Julian 5 points on the equation. List points with integer coefficients on the line.

   _____

9. Solve the system of equations: $y = 7x - 51$ and $y = -3x + 29$

   _____

10. Solve the system of equations: $y = -9x - 21$ and $y = 5x + 7$

    _____

Challenge Problems: Changing Words Into Symbols; Problem Solving With Equations (page 21)

1. $(2x - 6) + 9$
2. $3q + 75$
3. $x + (2x - 60°) = 180°$; 80° and 100°
4. $2(x + x + 1) = 3(x + 2) + 9$; 13, 14, and 15
5. $\dfrac{x}{x + 5}$; $\dfrac{x + 1}{(x + 5) - 3} = \dfrac{4}{5}$; $\dfrac{3}{8}$

Checking Progress: Solving Equations and Problems (page 22)

1. $12x - 15$
2. 0
3. $9x - 27$
4. $x = 15$
5. $x = 13$
6. $\dfrac{1}{19}$
7. $(x + 16) + x = 190$; 103 in grade 11; 87 in grade 12
8. $\$39.95 + 150x = \$72.95$; \$0.22
9. $\$340 + 14x = \$732$; 28 hours
10. $x + (2x - 2) + (0.5x + 7) = 180$; 50°, 98°, 32°

Practice: Inequalities (pages 27–29)

1. False
2. True
3. True
4. False
5. False
6. True
7. False
8. False
9. True
10. False
11. False
12. False
13. True
14. True
15. 2
16.

17.

18.

19.

20.

21.

22.

23.

24.

25.

26. $x < \dfrac{8}{3}$
27. $x > -4$
28. $x > -2$
29. $x > \dfrac{6}{5}$
30. $x \le -3$
31. $x > 1$
32. $x < \dfrac{3}{2}$
33. $x > 2$
34. $x < 2$
35. $x > 0$
36. $x > 0$
37. $x > -2$
38. $x > -2$
39. $x > -2$
40. $x > -2$
41. $x < 13$
42. $x < 9$
43. $x < 1.5$
44. $x < 1$

45. $x > -\frac{1}{6}$ or $x < \frac{1}{2}$. That is, x is any real number.
46. $-13 \leq x \leq 7$
47. $x \leq -17$ or $x \geq 7$
48. $x \leq -4$ or $x \geq 13$
49. $-8 \leq x \leq -4$
50. $x \leq -24$ or $x \geq 39$

-35 -30 -25 -20 -15 -10 -5 0 5 10 15 20 25 30 35 40 45 50

Challenge Problems: Inequalities (page 30)

1. True for all values of a
2. False
3. False
4. -4
5. $x < \frac{7}{3}$
6. $x < 2$
7. $x > 3$
8. No values are possible.
9. This is never true.
10. $x \leq -50$ or $x \geq 20$

Checking Progress: Inequalities (page 31)

1. False
2. False
3.

-11 -10 -9 -8 -7 -6 -5 -4 -3 -2 -1 0 1 2 3 4 5 6

4.

-9 -8 -7 -6 -5 -4 -3 -2 -1 0 1 2 3 4 5 6 7 8

5. $x < -6$
6. $x < -5$
7. $x < 19$
8. $x > -2$
9. $x \leq -10$ or $x \geq -6$
10. $-4 \leq x \leq 16$

Practice: Linear Equations and Graphs (pages 35–36)

1.

x	y
-2	7
-1	5
0	3
1	1
2	-1
5	-7
12	-21

2.

x	y
-2	-2
-1	1
0	4
1	7
2	10
5	19
12	40

3.

x	y
-2	10
-1	7
0	4
1	1
2	-2
5	-11
12	-32

4.

x	y
-2	-6
-1	-5.5
0	-5
1	-4.5
2	-4
5	-2.5
12	1

5.

x	y
-2	$-3\frac{1}{2}$
-1	$-2\frac{3}{4}$
0	-2
1	$-1\frac{1}{4}$
2	-0.5
5	$1\frac{3}{4}$
12	7

6.

x	y
-2	$3\frac{4}{5}$
-1	$3\frac{2}{5}$
0	3
1	$2\frac{3}{5}$
2	$2\frac{1}{5}$
5	1
12	$-1\frac{4}{5}$

111

7.

x	y
$\frac{22}{3}$	-5
$\frac{16}{3}$	-2
4	0
$\frac{10}{3}$	1
$\frac{188}{3}$	100

8.

x	y
1	-5
$\frac{12}{5}$	-2
2	0
$\frac{11}{5}$	1
22	100

14.

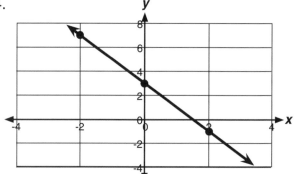

9.

x	y
$\frac{34}{4}$	-5
$\frac{19}{4}$	-2
$\frac{9}{4}$	0
1	1
$-\frac{491}{4}$	100

10.

x	y
$\frac{21}{6}$	-5
4	-2
$\frac{13}{3}$	0
$\frac{9}{2}$	1
$\frac{65}{3}$	100

15.

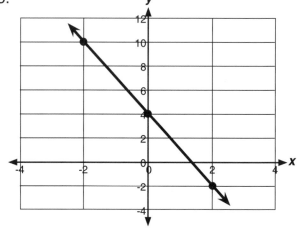

11.

x	y
$-\frac{1}{5}$	-5
$\frac{2}{5}$	-2
$\frac{4}{5}$	0
1	1
$\frac{194}{5}$	100

12.

x	y
$-\frac{50}{3}$	-5
$-\frac{35}{3}$	-2
$-\frac{25}{3}$	0
$-\frac{20}{3}$	1
$\frac{495}{3}$	100

16.

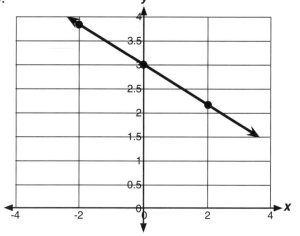

13.

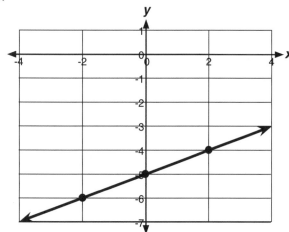

17.

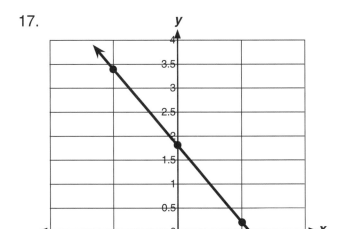

20.

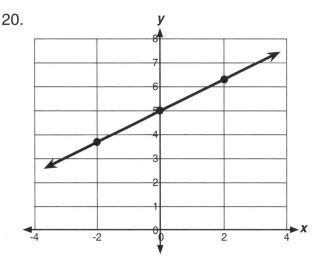

Challenge Problems: Linear Equations and Graphs (page 37)

1. She is correct. The *y*-intercept is where the *x* coordinate is zero.

2. Diane knows that the point (0, 5) tells her the *y*-intercept is 5. Using the two points (0, 5) and (2, 0) she can quickly determine the slope to be $-\frac{5}{2}$. Hence the equation for the line is $y = -\frac{5}{2}x + 5$.

3. Among the many things that Rachel might have noticed is that (0, 5) and (0, 9), (1, 8) and (1, 12), (2, 11) and (2, 15), etc. were solutions, respectively, to the equations. From this she might have said "given the same value of *x*, the *y* values in the second equation are always 4 more than the *y* values in the first equation," or "as *x* increases by 1, *y* increases by 3 for either equation."

4. Yes. These two equations are identical. Divide both sides of the second equation by two and you get the first equation [or multiply both sides of the first equation by two and you will get the second equation].

5. Erin was well versed with the idea of slope. From the equation $2x + 3y = 369$ she knew that the slope was $-\frac{2}{3}$. Using this she knew that (51, 89), (54, 87), (57, 85), (60, 83), etc. were points on the line. Erin might also have used (45, 93), (42, 95), (39, 97), and (36, 99).

18.

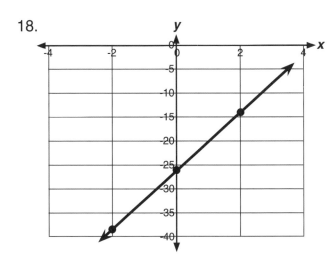

19.

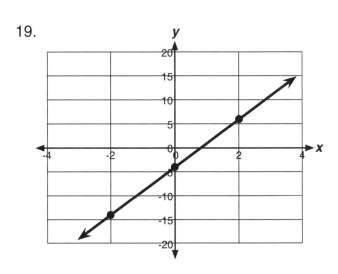

Practice: Linear Inequalities and Graphs (page 39)

1.

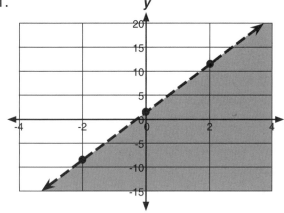

2.

3.

4.

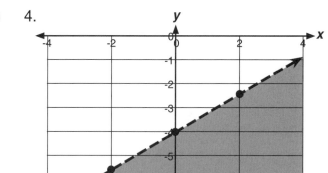

5.

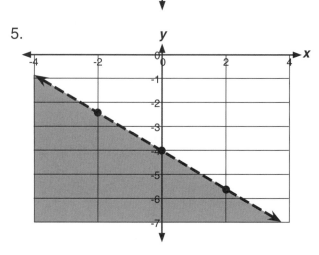

6.

7.

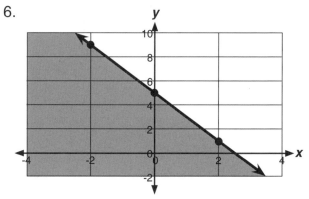

8.

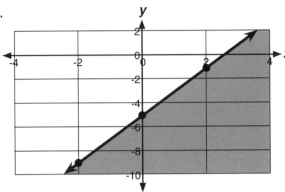

Note that this is the same line as in Question 7, but the regions shaded are opposite of each other.

Challenge Problems: Linear Inequalities (page 39)

1.

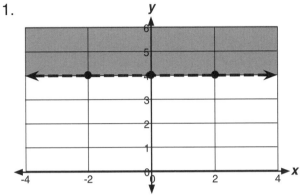

9.

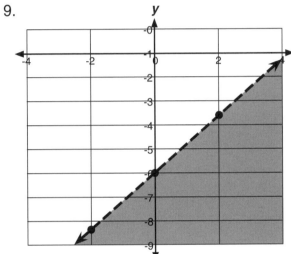

2.

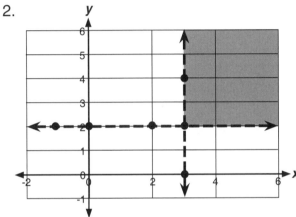

3.

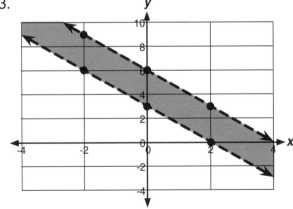

10.

Practice: Linear Systems (page 44)

1. (7, -2)
2. (2, 3)
3. (13, 2)
4. (8, 3)
5. (3, 8)

6. (1, 5)
7. (4, 1)
8. (1, 3)
9. (-5, 5)
10. (-1, -1)
11. (4, 7)
12. (92, 0)

Challenge Problems: Linear Systems (page 44)

1. There is no value that satisfies both equations.
2. (0.5, 0.5)
3. These lines are the same, so any ordered pair that satisfies one satisfies the other equation.

Checking Progress: Linear Equations and Inequalities (page 45)

1.

x	y
-2	-7
-1	-5
0	-3
1	-1
2	1
5	7
12	21

2.

x	y
-2	11
-1	8
0	5
1	2
2	-1
5	-10
12	-31

3.

x	y
-9.5	-5
-8	-2
-7	0
-6.5	1
43	100

4.
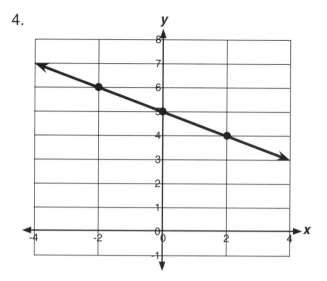

5.
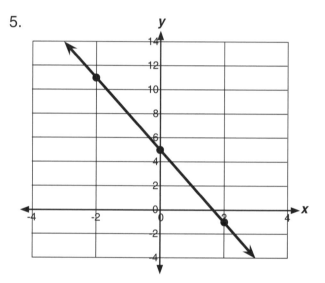

6.
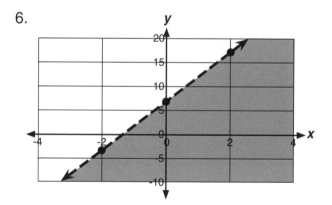

7.

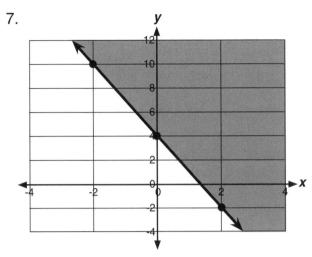

8. Some points are: (-7, 37), (-10, 57), (-13, 77), (-16, 97), (-1, -3), (2, -23), (5, -43)
9. (3, 5)
10. (-1, 3)

Practice: Simplifying Polynomials and Laws of Exponents (pages 47–48)

1. $-2x^2 + 11x - 6$
2. $15x^2 - 4x + 11$
3. $8x^3 + 4x^2 + 14x - 12$
4. $-x^3 - 7x^2 + 12x$
5. $-6x^3 + 4x^2 + 6x + 6$
6. $12x^3 + 4x^2 - 6x - 12$
7. $14x^3 - 4x^2 + 15x + 11$
8. $-16x^3 + 25x^2 + 9x + 3$
9. $6x^3 - 14x^2 - 18x + 3$
10. $-3x^3 - 10x^2 - 4x - 17$
11. $7x^3 + 2x^2 + 14x + 5$
12. $-4x^2 - 10$
13. $2.3x^3 + 6.3x^2 - 11.6x + 0.4$
14. $0.9x^3 - 1.1x^2 - 3x + 2.6$
15. $-0.6x^3 - 12.6x - 0.35$
16. $12a^4$
17. $18a^4$
18. $36a^4$
19. $12a^7b^7$
20. $405a^6$
21. $4a^7b^2$
22. $27a^6b^3c^9$
23. $0.000729a^6b^{12}$
24. $64a^8$
25. $12a^3b^3c^3d^5$

Challenge Problems: Simplifying Polynomials and Laws of Exponents (page 48)

1. $7x^3 + 2x^2 + 14x + 5$
2. $x^3 + x + 1$
3. $0.6x^3 + 12.6x + 0.35$
4. $3a$
5. $81a^{16}$

Practice: Multiplying and Factoring Polynomials (pages 50–51)

1. $2x^2 - 13x + 15$
2. $2x^2 - 13x + 15$
3. $x^3 - 1$
4. $x^4 + x^2 + 1$
5. $x^2 - 4xy + 4y^2$
6. $x^3 - 3x^2y + 2x + 2xy^2 - 4y$
7. $2x^4 - 13x^3 + 21x^2 - 39x + 45$
8. $x^3 + 3x^2 + 3x + 1$
9. $(3 - x)(3 + x)$
10. $(3x + 2y)^2$
11. $(10x - 7)(10x + 7)$
12. $(x + 4y)(x^2 - 4xy + 16y^2)$
13. $(4y - 5x)^2$
14. $(x^2 - y^2)(x^2 - y^2) = (x - y)^2(x + y)^2$
15. Cannot be factored with integer coefficients
16. $(1 - 2x)(3 + 5x)$ or equivalent such as $(2x - 1)(-3 - 5x)$

Challenge Problems: Multiplying and Factoring Polynomials (page 51)

1. $x^3 + 3x^2y + 3xy^2 + y^3$
2. $6x^2y + 2y^3$
3. $(x + 1)(x^2 - x + 1)$
4. $(a + b)(c + d)$
5. $(x^3 + y^3)(x^3 - y^3)$
   $= (x + y)(x^2 - xy + y^2)(x - y)(x^2 + xy + y^2)$
6. $[(x^2 + 2y^2) - 2xy][(x^2 + 2y^2) + 2xy]$

Practice: Solving Polynomial Equations (page 53)

1. $x = 4$ or $x = -3$
2. $x = -5$ or $x = -2$
3. $x = \frac{1}{2}$ or $x = -7$

4. $x = -\frac{2}{3}$ or $x = \frac{1}{5}$
5. No solution
6. $x = \frac{2}{5}$
7. $x = \frac{2}{5}$ or $x = -\frac{2}{5}$
8. $x^2 - 3x + 2 = 0$
9. 9 coins by 25 coins
10. 26 and 28

Challenge Problems: Solving Polynomials (page 53)

1. $y^2 = y + 12$
   Write the equation = to 0.
   $y^2 - y - 12 = y + 12 - y - 12$
   $y^2 - y - 12 = 0$
   Factor the other side.
   $(y + 3)(y - 4) = 0$
   Write each factor as an equation that is equal to 0.
   $y + 3 = 0 \qquad\qquad y - 4 = 0$
   Solve the equations.
   $y + 3 - 3 = 0 - 3 \quad y - 4 + 4 = 0 + 4$
   $y = -3 \qquad\qquad\quad y = 4$
   Check the answers in the original equation.
   $y^2 = y + 12 \qquad\qquad y^2 = y + 12$
   $-3^2 = -3 + 12 \qquad\quad 4^2 = 4 + 12$
   $9 = 9 \qquad\qquad\qquad 16 = 16$
   The solution set is {-3, 4}.

2. $x^2 = x + 30$
   Write the equation = to 0.
   $x^2 = x + 30$
   $x^2 - x - 30 = x + 30 - x - 30$
   $x^2 - x - 30 = 0$
   Factor the other side.
   $x^2 - x - 30 = 0$
   $(x + 5)(x - 6) = 0$
   Write each factor as an equation that is equal to 0.
   $x + 5 = 0 \qquad\qquad x - 6 = 0$
   Solve the equations.
   $x + 5 = 0 \qquad\qquad x - 6 = 0$
   $x + 5 - 5 = 0 - 5 \quad x - 6 + 6 = 0 + 6$
   $x = -5 \qquad\qquad\quad x = 6$

Check the answers in the original equation.
$x^2 = x + 30 \qquad\qquad x^2 = x + 30$
$(-5)^2 = -5 + 30 \qquad (6)^2 = 6 + 30$
$25 = 25 \qquad\qquad\quad 36 = 36$
Solution set is {-5, 6}.

Checking Progress: Polynomial Products and Factors (page 54)

1. $7x^3 - 11x^2 - 7x + 6$
2. $4.2x^3 - 0.6x + 1.15$
3. $0.064a^6b^{15}$
4. $8a^{24}b^2$
5. $8x^3 + 12x^2 + 6x + 1$
6. $x^4 + x^3y + 2x^2y + 2xy^2$
7. $(3x + 5)(3x - 7)$
8. $(4x + y)(16x^2 + 4xy + y^2)$
9. $x = -\frac{2}{5}$ or $x = -\frac{3}{4}$
10. Base is 40 inches and altitude is 32 inches.

Practice: Rational Expressions (pages 58–61)

1. $\dfrac{1}{5^8}$
2. $\dfrac{5^3}{7^2}$
3. $\dfrac{7y^4}{9}$
4. $2^{18}x^{18}$
5. 27
6. $27x^{12}$
7. 2^6
8. 2^7
9. $\dfrac{2^3 \bullet 3^5 \bullet 5^3}{7}$
10. $\dfrac{3 \bullet 7^5 \bullet 11^3}{2^2 \bullet 5^7}$
11. $\dfrac{5^2}{2^2 \bullet 3^4y^2}$
12. $\dfrac{1}{2}$
13. $1.22 \bullet 10^{-4}$
14. $3.45 \bullet 10$

15. $3.852 \cdot 10^8$
16. $3.5 \cdot 10^{-3}$
17. $4.41 \cdot 10^3$
18. 2,250,000
19. 0.00012
20. 4,600
21. 1,050
22. 0.00000042
23. $\dfrac{y + x}{xy}$
24. $\dfrac{2x}{(x - 2)(x + 2)}$
25. $\dfrac{4}{(x - 2)(x + 2)}$
26. $\dfrac{2x}{3}$
27. $\dfrac{1}{6}$
28. $\dfrac{15}{2xy^3}$
29. $\dfrac{50x^5}{27y^3}$
30. $\dfrac{5a^4}{3y^4}$
31. $\dfrac{37}{42}$
32. $\dfrac{29x + 77}{21}$
33. $\dfrac{10x^2 + 6x - 133}{21(x - 5)(x + 2)}$
34. $\dfrac{5x + 18}{2x^2 + x - 15}$
35. $\dfrac{18 - 5x}{2x^2 - x - 15}$
36. $\dfrac{4}{(x + 2)^2(x - 2)}$
37. $\dfrac{-4}{(x - 2)^2(x + 2)}$
38. $\dfrac{yz + xy + xz}{xyz}$
39. $\dfrac{7(x - 1)}{12y}$
40. $\dfrac{2a^2 + 3a + 1}{2(a^2 - 9)}$
41. $z = 4.8$

42. $x = 5$
43. $y = \dfrac{2}{5}$
44. $x = 7$
45. $x = 7$
46. This is true in all cases except when $x =$ -2.
47. $x = -3$
48. $x = 4$ or $x = -1$
49. $x = -7$
50. $x = 3$

Challenge Problems: Rational Expressions (page 62)
1. $1.44 \cdot 10^9$
2. 0.00000012
3. Wendy. 3^{2^3} is the same as 3^8 while 3^{3^2} is the same as 3^9.
4. $\dfrac{1}{2^7}$
5. $\dfrac{28x + 30y - 21z}{42}$
6. $\dfrac{8x + 9}{(x - 4)(x + 3)(x - 2)}$
7. $x = \dfrac{1}{3}$
8. $\dfrac{1}{3}$

Checking Progress: Rational Expressions (page 63)
1. $\dfrac{64y^4}{x}$
2. $\dfrac{3 \cdot 7^6 \cdot 11^3}{2 \cdot 5^{44}}$
3. $2.352 \cdot 10^{-3}$
4. 602,000
5. $\dfrac{250}{3y^2}$
6. $\dfrac{10x^2 + 36x + 77}{21(x + 2)(x + 5)}$
7. $x = -145$
8. No solution

Challenge Problems: Solving Quadratic Equations (page 88)

1. $0.084x^2 - 0.153x - 0.1425 = 0$
2. 1, -4
3. $\dfrac{0.82 \pm \sqrt{0.7924}}{0.4}$ or $2.05 \pm 5\sqrt{0.1981}$
4. Tanya is correct because the discriminant is negative.
5. If x is the width of the rectangle she is to build, then $32 - 2x$ is the length and $x(32 - 2x)$ is the equation that represents the area. The equation $x(32-2x)$ is equivalent to $-2x^2 + 32x$. When this equation is graphed, it forms a parabola that opens down. The x-coordinate of the vertex is 8. Hence, the fence with the largest area is made by an 8 x 16 rectangle.

Practice: Quadratic Functions and Graphs (pages 91–92)

1. Complete the table below:
   A.   Up   Narrow
   B.   Up   Wide
   C.   Down   Wide
   D.   Up   Narrow
   E.   Down   Narrow
   F.   Up   Narrow
   G.   Up   Narrow
   H.   Up   Narrow
   I.   Up   Wide
   J.   Down   Narrow
   K.   Down   Neither
2. For each quadratic function below, find the vertex for the parabola.
   A. (4, -1)   B. (-2, -3)
   C. (-1, 2)   D. (7, 35)
   E. $(-\frac{1}{2}, 3)$ F. $(\frac{2}{3}, -4)$
3. For each quadratic function, find the x-intercepts, if they exist.
   A. (0, 0), (-4, 0)   B. Do not exist
   C. Do not exist   D. (-3, 0), (1, 0)
   E. $\left(\dfrac{-3\pm\sqrt{19}}{2}, 0\right)$ F. (-2, 0), (5, 0)

4.

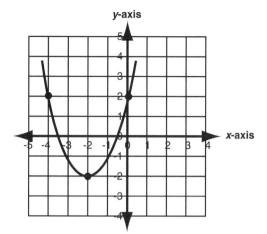

5.

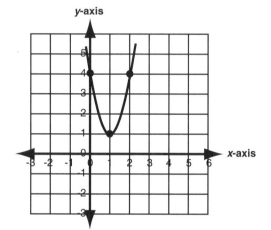

Challenge Problems: Quadratic Functions and Graphs (pages 92–93)

1. She is using the "b" term instead of the "a" term to determine which way the graph opens. She is also using the term wrong. She should look at the "a" term's sign. Also, she should check to see if the absolute value of the coefficient "a" is greater than 1 for narrow or between 0 and 1 for wide.
2. Galen is correct. Curtis used an incorrect formula and calculated the x-coordinate of the vertex to be the value of $\dfrac{2b}{a}$.
3. John is incorrect. This graph does have x-intercepts because the discriminant $(D = b^2 - 4ac = 33)$ is positive, indicating there are two real roots.
4. Variety of answers

Checking Progress: Quadratic Equations and Functions; Parabolas (pages 93–94)

1. $6x^2 - 2x = 0$ 2. $-2x^2 - 4x = 0$
3. $8x^2 - 2x - 1 = 0$
4. $-6x^2 + 13x - 6 = 0$

5. $-\frac{1}{2}, \frac{5}{4}$ 6. $\frac{1}{6}, -\frac{2}{3}$

7. $2, -4$ 8. $\frac{1}{6} \pm \frac{\sqrt{47}}{6}\, i$

9. $3, -\frac{1}{2}$

10. A.   Down   Neither
    B.   Down   Narrow

11. A. $(\frac{7}{4}, \frac{121}{8})$ B. $(\frac{1}{3}, \frac{14}{3})$
12. A. $(-4 + \sqrt{19}, 0), (-4 - \sqrt{19}, 0)$

    B. $\left(-\frac{3}{2} + \frac{\sqrt{105}}{6}, 0\right),$
$\left(-\frac{3}{2} - \frac{\sqrt{105}}{6}, 0\right)$

13.

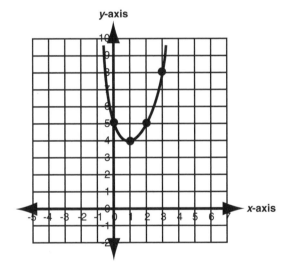

Practice: Variation (page 98)

1. 1.5 2. $\frac{75}{8}$

3. $\frac{20}{3}$ 4. 8
5. 72 6. 90

7. 12 8. $\frac{7}{2}$
9. 20 10. 5

11. $\frac{7}{6}$ 12. $\frac{15}{2}$
13. 56 14. 135

Challenge Problems: Direct Variation (page 99)

1. $\frac{5}{4}p$
2. Jim is not correct. $y = 2.5$ and $z = 5$
3. Jim is correct. $y = 40$ and $z = 20$
4. x is directly proportional to z.
   $x = ky$ and $y = mz \Rightarrow x = k(mz) = (km)z$

Checking Progress: Variation (page 99)

1. 4 2. $\frac{1500}{16}$, or $\frac{375}{4}$
3. 80 4. 2

5. $\frac{1}{75}$ 6. 1

7. $\frac{1}{2}$ 8. 100

9. $\frac{28}{5}$ 10. $2p$

Check-up Problems Answer Keys

Check-up Problems: Solving Equations and Problems (page 100)

1. $4x + 26$ 2. 0
3. $7 - 3x$ 4. $x = -3$
5. $x = -3$ 6. $x = 3$
7. 420 boys, 480 girls   8. $0.30 per min.
9. 30 hours   10. $24°, 50°, 106°$

Check-up Problems: Inequalities (page 101)

1. False   2. True
3.

4.

5. $x < 2$ 6. $x > 0.5$
7. $x < 29$
8. True for all real numbers

9. $x \leq -\frac{7}{3}$ or $x \geq 7$ 10. $-35 \leq x \leq 20$

Check-up Problems: Linear Equations and Inequalities (pages 102–103)

1.

x	y
-2	-23
-1	-18
0	-13
1	-8
2	-3
5	12
12	47

2.

x	y
-2	23
-1	18
0	13
1	8
2	3
5	-12
12	-47

3.

x	y
1	-5
-2	-2
-4	0
-5	1
-104	100

4.

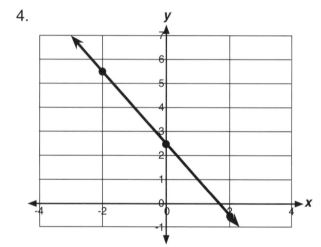

5.

6.

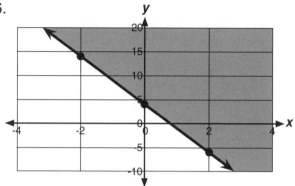

7.

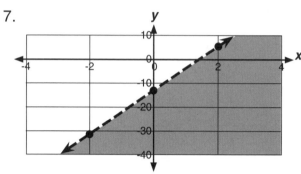

8. (-1, 201), (-10, 401), (-19, 601), (-28, 801), (17, -199), (26, -399), (35, -599), etc.
9. (8, 5)
10. (-2, -3)

Check-up Problems: Polynomial Products and Factors (page 104)

1. $-8x^2 + 10x + 5$
2. $6x^3 + 7x^2 - 10x - 35$
3. $a^{10}b^9c^7$
4. $0.0625a^6b^{12}$
5. $2x^2 + 2ax - bx - ab$
6. $x^2 - 4y^2$
7. $(2x - 5)(5x - 2)$
8. $(x + y)(x^2 - xy + y^2)$
9. $x = \frac{2}{5}$ or $x = -\frac{3}{7}$
10. The width is 18 inches, and the length is 28 inches.

Check-up Problems: Rational Expressions (page 105)

1. $\dfrac{112x^2}{3y^2}$

2. $\dfrac{2^2 \cdot 5^7}{3 \cdot 7^5 \cdot 11^3}$

3. $2.035 \cdot 10^6$

4. 0.00123

5. $\dfrac{7x}{27y}$

6. $\dfrac{3x^2 + 2x - 43}{4(x-5)(x-2)}$

7. $x = \dfrac{-10}{3}$

8. $x = 5$ or $x = -1$

9. $\dfrac{12x - 70y - 21z}{42}$

10. $\dfrac{13}{21}$

Check-up Problems: Roots, Radicals, and Complex Numbers (page 106)

1. $\dfrac{b^3}{2y^2}\sqrt[4]{y^2}$

2. $\dfrac{1}{3}\sqrt{6}$

3. $6\sqrt{2}$

4. $25 - 22\sqrt{2}$

5. $4\sqrt{3} - 7$

6. $x = 8$

7. $x = \dfrac{3}{2}$ or $\dfrac{-1}{2}$

8. $0.\overline{538461}$

9. $11 + 23i$

10. $\dfrac{3 - 4i}{5}$

Check-up Problems: Quadratic Equations and Functions (page 107)

1. $x^2 - x = 0$
2. $-12x^2 - 84x = 0$
3. $x^2 - 1 = 0$
4. $-x^2 + 6x - 9 = 0$
5. $8, -9$
6. $\dfrac{7}{2}, -\dfrac{9}{7}$
7. $-3 \pm \sqrt{23}$
8. $1, -3$
9. Complete the table below:
   A.   Down   Wide
   B.   Up   Narrow
10. $(2, 6)$

11. $\left(-1 + \dfrac{\sqrt{6}}{2}, 0\right), \left(-1 - \dfrac{\sqrt{6}}{2}, 0\right)$

12.

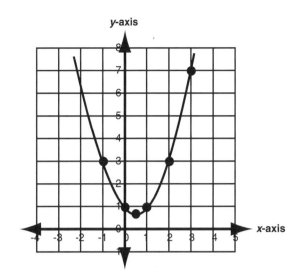

Check-up Problems: Variation (page 108)

1. 40
2. 75
3. 5,600
4. 2
5. $\dfrac{1}{750}$
6. 100
7. $\dfrac{1}{2}$
8. 100
9. 4
10. $pm/4$

125

References

Brown, R., Dolciani, M., Sorgenfrey, R., Cole, W., (1997). *Algebra structure and method book 1.* Evanston, IL: McDougal Littell.

Chicago Mathematics Project. *Connected mathematics.* University of Chicago. Found online at: http://www.math.msu.edu/cmp/curriculum/Algebra.htm

Edwards, E. (1990). *Algebra for everyone.* Reston, VA: National Council of Teachers of Mathematics.

Long, L. (1998). *Painless algebra.* Hauppauge, NY: Barron's Educational Series.

National Council for Teachers of Mathematics. (2000). *Principles and standards for school mathematics.* Reston, VA: National Council of Teachers of Mathematics.

National Council of Teachers of Mathematics (NCTM). (2004). *Standards and expectations for algebra.* Reston, VA: National Council of Teachers of Mathematics. Found online at: http://www.nctm.org

Freudenthal Institute at the University of Utrecht/University of Wisconsin/NSF. *Math in context.* Found online at http://showmecenter.missouri.edu/showme/mic.shtml Encyclopedia Britannica.

Web Resources

Reichman, H. and Kohn, M. (2004). *Math made easy.* Found Online at: http://www.mathmadeeasy.com/algebra.html

Algebra.help. (2001–2004). *Algebra help.* Found online at: http://www.algebrahelp.com/index.jsp

Algebra Solutions
http://www.gomath.com/algebra.html

Brennon, J. (2002). *Understanding algebra.* Found online at: http://www.jamesbrennan.org/algebra/

Classzone Algebra 1
http://www.classzone.com/books/algebra_1/index.cfm

Math Archives: Topics in Mathematics Algebra
http://www.archives.math.utk.edu/topics/algebra.html

Math for Morons Like Us
http://library.thinkquest.org/20991/alg2/

Reliable problem solving in all subjects that use mathematics for problem solving. Algebra, Physics, Chemistry … from grade school to grad school and beyond.
http://www2.hawaii.edu/suremath/intro_algebra.html

The Math Forum Drexel University (1994–2004). *K–12 Internet Algebra Resources.* Philadelphia, PA: Found online at: http://mathforum.org/algebra/k12.algebra.html

Borenson, H. (2001–2004). *Hands on Equations.* Allentown, PA: Borenson and Associates. Found online at: http://www.borenson.com

Oracle Education Foundation Think Quest Library (2004). *Algebra.* Found online at: http://library.thinkquest.org/10030/algecon.htm

Oswego Public Schools
http://regentsprep.org/Regents/math/variation/Ldirect.htm

Oswego Public Schools Teacher Resource Page—Direct Variation
http://regentsprep.org/Regents/math/variation/Tdirect.htm

University of Akron Theoretical and Applied Mathematics
http://www.math.uakron.edu/~dpstory/mpt_home.html

Ed Helper.com
http://www.edhelper.com/algebra.htm

Introduction to Algebra
http://www.mathleague.com/help/algebra/algebra.htm

History of Algebra
http://www.ucs.louisiana.edu/~sxw8045/history.htm

Surfing the Net With Kids
http://www.surfnetkids.com/algebra.htm

Moses, B. *The algebra project.* Cambridge, MA: The Algebra Project, Inc. Found online at: http://algebra.org/index.html

Interactive Mathematic Miscellany and Puzzles
http://www.cut-the-knot.org/algebra.shtml

Awesome Library—Algebra
http://www.awesomelibrary.org/Classroom/Mathematics/Middle-High_School_Math/Algebra.html

Cool Math Sites
http://www.cte.jhu.edu/techacademy/web/2000/heal/mathsites.htm

SOS Mathematics
http://www.sosmath.com/

Real Life Applications of Math

Applied Academics: Applications of Mathematics—Careers
http://www.bced.gov.bc.ca/careers/aa/lessons/math.htm

Exactly How Is Math Used in Technology?
http://www.math.bcit.ca/examples/index.shtml

Mathematics Association of America—Careers
http://www.maa.org/careers/index.html

NASA Space Link
http://spacelink.msfc.nasa.gov/index.html